Daybreak
with
Jesus

Daybreak
with
Jesus

Daily Devotions from the
Sermon on the Mount to Equip Us
to Love God and Our Neighbor

BURTIS WILLIAMS

LIFEWISE BOOKS

Daybreak with Jesus
Daily Meditations from the Sermon on the Mount
by
BURTIS WILLIAMS

———————————

All Greek and Hebrew definitions come from Strong's Exhaustive Concordance of the Bible.

PUBLISHED BY:

⊕ LIFEWISE BOOKS
PO BOX 1072
Pinehurst, TX 77362
LifeWiseBooks.com

To contact the author: burtisdw@gmail.com

ISBN (Print): 978-1-952247-86-6
ISBN (Ebook): 978-1-952247-87-3

Dedication

To Linda—my wife, companion, and faithful partner in the service of our Lord Jesus Christ for almost sixty years.

Special Acknowledgments

Dr. E. Harold Henderson (deceased)
and
Dr. T. C. Melton
whose mentorships are reflected to a substantial degree in this book.

Contents

Introduction

It has been said that a picture is worth a thousand words. I beg to differ. Nothing creates vision like the well-spoken or well-written word. In my imagination, I have traveled the world since the days of my youth. It is in the mind's eye where scenes, smells, and "reality" is created. The soft, warm breezes and transparent waters of the South Pacific, the vast Serengeti of Africa, the poverty and deprivation of some third world countries, the marvel of the Austrian Alps, the ancient sites of the Holy Land, the ruins of Rome,the list is endless. Most of us have known the disappointment of the pale representation of a great book when it appears in the film. As good as a picture is, nothing compares to the human mind; the imagination is excited by the picture painted with expressive words of a good text.

Where would we be without the Ten Commandments, Washington's farewell message to the nation at the end of his presidency, or the Gettysburg Address? Add the Sermon on the Mount (the subject of this study) and combine all these documents, and you still hardly have a thousand words.

I have chosen to take the most remarkable exposition of the greatest concepts ever heard in the human experience, and offer a few thoughts about them. The "Sermon on the Mount" is without parallel in human history. In Matthew 5-7, the collective wisdom of all the ages is summarized by the greatest Teacher who ever has, or shall, live. In words a junior high school student could understand, Jesus set forth the meaning of the most transforming truths ever presented on earth.

The Structure of This Book

I spend an hour or so researching and writing after finishing my quiet time. I developed this study by taking a verse or section of the sermon and mining for every bit of truth I could find in the text itself. I investigated each word or phrase as to its meaning in the original languages. I tried to state the literal meaning so the ordinary Christian could understand and apply it. Let me be clear. My conviction is that the Bible in general (and the teachings of Jesus in particular) are to be accepted literally unless the context obviously intends a different meaning. To use a common conservative phrase for interpreting Scripture: "When the plain sense of Scripture makes common sense, seek no other sense."

I have but a meager acquaintance with the Greek and Hebrew languages. I am so grateful for those who know those languages thoroughly and for the helpful tools developed for those with significant limitations like me. I've designed each entry in such a way that it could be your devotional (or part of it) for the day.

One more thing. It has always been helpful to me if I could see the truth in scripture lived out in the life of an ordinary Christian. Within the pages of Christian history, inspirational and encouraging stories abound as to the faithfulness of God's chosen ones. Those whose overcoming stories are told in the text of Scripture are joined by countless ones who now have entered the cloud of witnesses who observe us. I have sought out Christian responses in real life to illustrate what a given text in the Sermon on the Mount is teaching. In the way these saints responded to their time of challenge, I pray you will find the truth of the text more deeply anchored in your soul.

THE "SERMON ON THE MOUNT"

I do not believe the entire text of Matthew 5-7—the Sermon on the Mount—was spoken in one setting, in one detailed address on the hillside overlooking the Sea of Galilee. It is not a sermon as we think of a sermon, but a collection of His teachings. Jesus spoke every word in the Sermon on the Mount. They are all true, inspired, and inerrant. The Sermon on the Mount is the greatest collection of truth ever heard by man. The messages of this incomparable text are absolutely transforming and should be read by every Christian in their entirety regularly.

It is my conviction that Matthew, under the Spirit's leading, compiled the teachings of Jesus into these three chapters. From various settings with different audiences, Matthew captured the teaching of Jesus in each of those instances and assembled them here. We are forever indebted.

The opening of Matthew 5 describes the setting in which Jesus taught. This event overlooking the Sea of Galilee happened. Jesus did sit down—the position a rabbi took when he was about to deliver an official, authoritative message. He spoke directly to his disciples, and by extension, to others present and to all people of all time. The text says He "taught" them. The most common title attributed to Jesus was "Teacher." There is no nobler profession.

How much of the text of the three chapters He taught in the seaside setting, I do not know. It is enough for us to have the essence of all

He taught during the more than three years He walked the earth. The summary statement for all of us who follow Jesus is contained in Matthew 7:24-27. Jesus says that it is not the hearing of the words but the obedience of the heart that matters. So, in practical terms, each time you come to this study, you will see these three questions:

What does Jesus want me to know?

Why does He want me to know this?

What does He want me to do in response?

(At the end of each section, you are challenged to personally apply what God is saying to you. PLEASE respond to the three questions and take your responses with you into the day...and your life)

Let this be your heart's focus every morning. Before you begin your quiet time, pray for neutrality, discernment, and a teachable spirit, using these three questions. Do your quiet time. Meditate. Your most significant benefit will come if you discipline yourself to record what the Spirit reveals to you in your journal.

The Human Author of the Sermon on the Mount

Being a man familiar with detail and order as a tax collector, Matthew (Levi) is very orderly and sequential in how he writes. How he organized the details of the teaching and ministry of Jesus may have come from the orderly, sequential way Jesus did His public ministry. For example, His dismantling of Satan's temptations in the wilderness shows a pattern Jesus would use throughout the three years of His public ministry. In His response to Satan, we conclude that Jesus would focus everything He would do upon the absolute necessity of the cross.

Knowing His time was limited to initiate and sustain His worldwide, to-the-end-of-time ministry, Jesus had to choose those who would carry on after He returned to the Father. He chose twelve very ordinary men. The spiritual destiny of humankind would be entrusted to them. The twelve had to continue what He had begun—taking the good news to the entire world. He must teach/train them well. What He taught them, Matthew distills into three magnificent chapters.

The teachings of Jesus Matthew records begin with the "beatitudes." These are to be the essence of what a Christian is/does. The rest of the chapters will illuminate and extend what a follower of Jesus will be/do. There are numerous teaching methods. Some teaching is done by walking about, discussing what is encountered. Jesus did some teaching this way, often as parables. There is the method of teaching characterized by question/debate. When a rabbi was about deliver a formal address, he sat down. . Everyone understood: pay attention; something significant is about to be presented.

Overlooking the Sea of Galilee, Jesus sat down to teach. What He was about to say was: 1) official, dignified, weighty, and 2) it came from His heart. It was intimate, direct, and to be received with utmost seriousness. This is the real deal, disciples- "get" this!

If the phrase "He opened His mouth and taught them..." had been in the aorist tense, it would have referred to **an action that has happened in the past, has been completed, and is not to be repeated.** But the phrase is in the *imperfect tense* in the language. **The *imperfect tense* speaks of action initiated and continuing: This has <u>been</u> done, it is <u>being</u> done, it <u>is to be done indefinitely</u>.** See how important the tenses are?

Jesus taught the Sermon on the Mount in the *imperfect tense.* This is one reason to believe that He repeatedly taught these beatitudes throughout His ministry. Effective teaching requires repetition. Any person who teaches as a profession knows that many reminders and repetitions of content are necessary for the message to be grasped and applied.

So let's dive into these chapters. I pray you will find more than a surface, feel-good thought in each section. Instead, I pray you will find some "meat" of the Word, and your faith and practice will grow as you apply what the Spirit brings to your mind from your study through *Daybreak with Jesus.*

Day One

"Blessed are the poor in spirit for theirs is the kingdom of heaven."

MATTHEW 5:3

The "law of first mention" is important in Scripture. When a subject is first introduced in the Bible, take note; it is significant. This is the first time the "beatitudes" appear as such. Each of the beatitudes takes the same form. In each of them, the word "*are*" is in italics meaning that the word does not appear in the original text but is added to make the sense clearer to the average reader.

In their language of the day; Jesus addressed the disciples and the crowd–Aramaic. For our purposes, understand the Aramaic language is Greek with shades of the Hebrew incorporated into it. He said, "O the blessedness of the one..." This is precisely what Psalm 1:1 is saying, "Blessed is the one who walks not in the counsel of the ungodly..." He is describing a blessedness that is for the here and now.

By the grace of God, such blessedness is the present and continuing state of those who "get" the message Jesus is teaching. "Blessed" is *makarios* the thrill and radiance of being one of God's own. It is a joy that is dependent on nothing external. Blessedness is a serene, untouchable-by-circumstances condition. In loss, sorrow, grief, or pain—this joy sustains us. This state is not some distant, hoped-for state but a present reality in the real world in real-time. How could that be?!

"Blessed are the poor in spirit..." seems odd and illogical, doesn't it? It seems stranger still that, of beatitudes, this one would be stated first. The serene, undeterred-by-the-circumstances of life are found in the poor in spirit. What does this mean?

Two Greek words are translated as "poor" *penes* and *ptochos*. A man who is *penes* works with his hands. He lives hand-to-mouth. There are no extras, just enough to keep body and soul together. The *ptochos* man is totally, absolutely destitute. He has nothing...nothing; except, perhaps, the rags on his back. A word related to *ptochos* carries the thought of cowering, crouching, beaten to his knees. He is a beggar, totally without resources. His only recourse is to beg and pray for the mercy of others.

We noted earlier that Jesus taught in Aramaic, using words that were a blend between the Greek and the Hebrew. This helps us understand "poor" even better. In Aramaic there is a progression of the word "poor." First, it meant simply poor, the meaning we naturally associate with it. Then it came to include that, due to being poor, the person had no influence, power, or "say." Finally, poor came to mean that because they lived hand-to-mouth with zero extra, powerless, and without influence, they were downtrodden and oppressed by others.

The bottom line for the word "poor" in this beatitude meant that (having zero in things, influence, or "say" in anything) the poor man was left with God, alone. His only hope rested in God coming to his rescue. He had to trust God for EVERYTHING.

Repeatedly, in the Psalms, God's love and provision for the poor are stated. (See Psalm 34:6, 35:10, 68:10, 74:2, 132:15.) The Proverbs often speak of the poor and God's response to those who are compassionate toward them. The poor in spirit approach God in total surrender and trust.

Blessed is the person who realizes he has absolutely nothing to offer to God; one who knows he has no ground for gaining any standing whatsoever with God. He is utterly helpless. Detaching himself from anything he might find on earth to recommend him and attaching himself to God by simple faith. This is the person who is blessed.

> *"Nothing in my hand I bring*
> *Simply to Thy cross I cling..."* [1]

The very first beatitude establishes the truth upon which the remaining beatitudes will rest. The only ones who can blessedly move through life with quiet, utter confidence are those who have surrendered to God and look to Him for everything. Things, abilities, prestige... these mean nothing. God is everything.

The gospel is God's response to the poor in spirit. The gospel declares that all humankind is totally destitute of merit for salvation (Romans 3:23). Separation from God is man's natural state, and that separation is total. Bargaining with God is impossible. The poor have nothing with which to bargain. The result is that man, in his natural state, is destined to eternal separation from God in a place called hell (Romans 6:23a). BUT, realizing and acting upon his realization that he is totally dependent upon God's mercy and grace, the poor in spirit surrenders to God. At that moment of repentance and faith (surrender), the poor in spirit receive the gift of eternal life (Romans 6:23b).

With the blessed gift of salvation, the poor in spirit join the most significant cause on earth: that His will be done on earth as it is being done in heaven. Blessed is the person who has accepted their utter helplessness to gain standing with God. Blessed is the person who surrenders to Him for whatever He wills. And, in that same spirit of trust and surrender which brought salvation, partner with God to do His will, whatever that might mean. In every circumstance, the poor in spirit look to God, fully confident that He is both able and committed to being the solution to every circumstance. Trust and obey! Every other aspect of the Christian life is based on the meaning of this first beatitude. On the same basis as the Christian life begins, it will continue to the end of time.

A Pretty Girl, An Ugly Truck and Mr. Prigden

Johnny Hunt found himself facing the exact position which is described in this first beatitude. Johnny was being reared by a mom who worked two jobs to support her family. He was well on his way to a severe drinking problem by the time he was thirteen. Lacking adult supervision, he began skipping school and hanging out at a local pool hall; he dropped out of school at age sixteen. Playing pool five to eight hours a day, he became so good at pool that he was made the pool hall manager.

Taking an additional part-time job at a hardware store, Johnny managed to buy an old junker which he drove only when he had to because it was so ugly. He caught a ride with a friend to get back and forth to work most of the time. His friend was in a hurry one day, so he dropped Johnny off a few blocks home. Walking home, he saw a beautiful girl twirling a baton in her front yard. He had his friend drop him off every day after that so he could walk by that girl's house and catch a glimpse of her. He got a chance to meet her, and a year later, Johnny and Jan were married.

Johnny's wife was a Christian, and she wanted them to be active in a church. Johnny wasn't interested. About that same time, Mr. Prigden, who often came to the hardware store where Johnny worked, took an interest in Johnny. Every time Johnny checked Mr. Prigden out, he had something to say about his church and the good things that happened there. He often encouraged Johnny to come. Finally, Johnny gave in.

After attending Mr. Prigden's church a while, Johnny found himself experiencing something strange. He did just fine during the singing and preaching, but somehow when the pastor called for an invitation, Johnny felt very nervous, uncomfortable. Something inside was extraordinarily troubling, and he even got emotional during the invitation time. It was the work of the Holy Spirit drawing him to Jesus, but Johnny didn't understand that. In the morning service on January 7, 1973, his wife noticed his tears and questioned him, but he didn't know how to explain what was happening.

That afternoon, Johnny suddenly announced that they were going back to the church that night. He told Jan that he realized he had messed up his life, and though he had tried to clean it up, it wasn't working. If Jesus Christ could change my life, he said, He is welcome to it. Jan was astounded and delighted. They went to church that night, and Johnny surrendered his life to Jesus during the invitation.

From that moment on, Johnny was a changed man. He immediately began seeking out all of his old friends at the various hangouts where he had gained a reputation. "What are you going to do now that you are a Christian?" a skeptical friend asked. "I'm going to heaven and take as many with me as I can," Johnny replied.

Johnny went back and finished high school, then college, and then seminary. He found that Jesus could, indeed, change his life. Johnny went on to be one of the leading pastors in the Southern Baptist Convention, known for his great compassion and burden for those who did not know Jesus. Sharing the gospel was, and is, the centerpiece of his ministry. "Jesus took me from the poolroom to the pulpit through the influence of an ugly car, a beautiful girl, and Mr. Prigeden. He changed my life, and he can change yours. Johnny continues his efforts today to in a leadership position in the Southern Baptist Convention seeking to "...take as many to heaven with him as I can." [2]

What does Jesus want me to know?

Why does He want me to know this?

What does He want me to do in response?

Day Two

"Blessed are those who mourn for they shall be comforted."

MATTHEW 5:4

Life on earth will forever involve mourning. The word used here is the strongest term possible for mourning. It relates to the death of the most precious thing one has on earth. It is important to note that Jesus did not say, "Blessed are those who grieve." Grieving ones rarely find comfort; mourners do. What is the difference between grieving and mourning? Grieving is the internal thoughts and feelings one has about a significant loss. Mourning is the external expression of those thoughts and feelings one has in a loss. One is internal, and the other is external. If the response to a death is internalized, the loss is confined to the one grieving. It is only when one is trusting enough to share their grief that comforters appear.

When the pain of a death cannot be contained and hidden any longer, two things often occur:

1. Some other people who have experienced a death and know how difficult a loss can be will quietly step alongside the one grieving and say, "I know what it's like." To be sure, some wisdom must be applied to discern who would be the

appropriate one with whom to share. They are out there. Find them. Your loss is unique, but some understand more than you know.

2. Paul addressed this very thing in II Corinthians 1:3-4. When such a one says, "I know," you just know they do. They comfort you. Blessed are those who, in their deep sorrow, discover the sheer goodness and compassion of true friends. Then, allow them to walk with them to share the grief.

3. Blessed are those who mourn because the One "...who shares our sorrows and is acquainted with our grief..." is only a prayer away. I'm not sure how He does it, but in a way that is real and deeply meaningful, Jesus manifests His love and assurance when we go to Him in our mourning. A deeper and more meaningful fellowship with our Savior comes when we lean into Him and allow Him to draw us near in His gentle embrace. What joy when we experience Him in mourning.

The poor in spirit are often the ones who are the first ones to respond to another in grief and comforts in times of mourning. Knowing what it is like to feel destitute and hopeless, these experienced ones display authenticity. They feel blessed to get to companion one in mourning. In time, you, the mourner (now being comforted by a fellow traveler), will become the one who comforts. There is great satisfaction in comforting.

One final thought. In times of mourning, many see the cross and what happened there most graphically. It breaks the heart of many who have been indifferent to the awfulness of sin. That is why the poor in spirit must be alert and responsive. One never knows what will break the hard-hearted. To comfort a fellow traveler is one of the supreme joys in life—even if they don't turn toward the Savior. Gently, compassionately share the gospel-the message that reached us when we were totally destitute. Only eternity will show the impact of those who stood faithful, even to death.

A Devastating Loss In A Foreign Land

This message of eternal life was the heartbeat of the great missionary Adoniram Judson. He was sharing it throughout Burma when one of his many periods of anguish befell him. Judson had already buried a son in Burma, where he and his wife, Ann, were missionaries. He had also barely survived a seventeen-month imprisonment, one of the most horrifying experiences of his life. In 1826, he was called upon by the British government to negotiate with the Burmese king, a task that took some months. As he prepared to return to his family, anxious because Ann had been very sick, he received a letter which informed him that Ann had passed to her reward.

Judson was devastated, but he wrote Ann's mother a touching tribute to her beloved daughter. Not wishing to add to her sorrow, he refrained from sharing hisdevastation. He stated that he would provide additional details regarding her death as he was able. Most of his letter to Mrs. Hasseltine focused on Ann's relief from the pain and sorrow she had suffered and the blessed rest she now enjoyed with Jesus.

He wrote to Mrs. Hasseltine (Ann's mother) again the next spring. Additional sorrow had come to the faithful missionary. He had just buried his precious little daughter, Maria, who was just two years old. He shared that every effort had been made to save his beloved little girl, but to no avail. He buried Maria beside her mother in the small enclosure that had become the family cemetery. Little Maria joined her mother precisely six months after her mother's death.

Judson was left alone, far from home and family. He reflected on the fact that the life of a missionary—especially in a place as primitive as Burma—was difficult. He had now buried one in Rangoon and two in Amherst. He determined he would carry on and prepare himself to join his loved ones when, in God's good time, his time came to depart.[3]

What does Jesus want me to know?

Why does He want me to know this?

What does He want me to do in response?

Day Three

"Blessed are the meek for they shall inherit the earth."

MATTHEW 5:5

As we have realized, these simply stated principles Jesus spoke have profound meanings. On the surface, the beatitudes may seem to be a bit bland or confusing. But when one digs in, the deeper meaning of each beatitude emerges. This is especially true when one realizes that word meanings often change. Also, the words Jesus spoke have a richness the English language often does not confer. This is the case with this beatitude which centers on the word "meek."

In the culture of our day, to be meek means to be spineless or submissive. Especially in the west, we champion the two-fisted, take-no-prisoners attitude. Jesus taught that meekness is far stronger and more meaningful than that. The Greek word *praus* and the shades of meaning associated with it paint a picture of meekness that is almost the opposite of our cultural definition.

Two Greek words were used to define meekness, and they help us understand what Jesus said. These two words are both related to *praus* and were used by Aristotle for meek. He taught that meekness is the happy medium between excessive anger and excessive absence of anger. Neither extreme is acceptable. Meekness is balanced or properly disciplined anger.

So, we may restate the beatitude this way: "Blessed is the person who is angry at the right time, in the right way, in the right amount and is never angry at the wrong time, in the wrong way, in the wrong amount." Anger is the appropriate response to injustice or injury.

This (and all beatitudes) connects to the poor in spirit. Jesus is increasingly deepening His teaching. The person who is poor in spirit mourns when they encounter injustice or injury to an innocent party. Injury or injustice to oneself might be quickly and quietly handed over to God for His response by the poor in spirit, but the innocent are without an advocate. Blessed is the person who stands with and advocates for the innocent in the presence of injustice or injury. This is the first meaning for "Blessed are the meek..."

A second meaning for *praus* can be understood by the work of the "horse whisperer." Popular TV programs feature the horse whisperer stepping into an arena with a mustang fresh off the open range. The mustang has never had any dealings with a human, a rope, or any discipline. Wild with the "bit between the teeth," the mustang is accustomed to doing exactly as it pleases. The horse whisperer goes to work, and in a matter of hours, the mustang is "broken." Not broken in spirit but disciplined, controlled, and content to follow the guidance of a gentle but firm rider.

The mustang illustrates man in his natural state—wild, self-centered, the bit between his teeth...the center and circumference of his own life. The natural man does not receive the things of God. But when Jesus comes into the arena and a natural man admits to the impossibility of attaining a life of blessedness by his efforts, things change. In surrendering to Jesus and submitting to His control and discipline, the born-again one finds what he could never find in a thousand lifetimes: blessedness!

Self-control is not natural. To a limited degree and in limited ways, one may exercise some level of self-control. But legitimate self-control is impossible as a way of life for the unbeliever. That is why one of the fruits of the spirit is self-control. Only by being God-controlled can one be self-controlled. So, let's add to our understanding of this beatitude and state it this way: "Blessed is the person whose every impulse, thought, and passion is under control by submission to the Holy Spirit."

Let's go on to a third thought: *praotes,* forgiveness. Forgiveness means to release, remit or send away. It describes a person who humbly realizes the need to learn how to release a wrong done to them. Without this understanding, it is easy to become imbalanced, excusing what is inexcusable and being critical of what is personally displeasing. The first step in learning anything is to realize that everyone is ignorant-...just about different things. Blessed is the person who admits he doesn't know it all but tends to act as he does. The meek seek the wisdom and encouragement of those wiser than they. The meek understand that they do not need to have an opinion on every subject. The meek have enough self-control to realize when to release, remit, or send away a wrong done to themselves. This release is possible by knowing God will perfectly deal with any wrong in precisely the right way at the right time.

When we combine the shades of meaning in the word Jesus used for "meek" we understand how a person in leadership with this quality rises to the top of the leadership pyramid. "How blessed is the person who is angry at the right time, in the right way, and to the right degree. One whose every thought, passion, and impulse is under control and is humble enough to acknowledge his ignorance and tendencies to unforgiveness. Such a person will be a leader and a testimony."

Victory Out Of The Ashes

I know of no more remarkable example of one who grasped this beatitude than the "father of modern missions", William Carey. This truly remarkable man who had little formal education learned dozens of languages and dialects, especially those related to his beloved India, where he served as a missionary from 1793 to 1834. He did not take a single furlough in all that time. He was driven to give the Indians the gospel in their native language and dialect.

He established a large printing shop in Serampore, a two hundred by fifty feet building housing twenty translators. There, Carey supervised the creation of the first printing press in India. In addition, typesetters, compositors, pressmen, binders, and other writers assembled to translate and print the gospel in as many languages and dialects as possible, as quickly as possible.

On March 11, 1812, Carey was teaching in Calcutta when an associate brought him the devastating news that the entire building and all its contents except five pieces of equipment were destroyed by fire. Gone was Carey's entire library, his completed Sanskrit dictionary, part of his Bengal dictionary, two grammar books, and ten translations of the Bible. Ashes. Gone also were the type sets for printing fourteen different languages, vast quantities of paper, priceless dictionaries, deeds, and account books. All gone in a matter of hours.

Returning to Serampore and surveying the smoldering ruins, Carey wept. Then he said, "In one short evening, the labours of years are consumed. How unsearchable are the ways of God I had lately brought some things to the utmost perfection of which they seemed capable and contemplated the missionary establishment with perhaps too much self-congratulations. The Lord has laid me low, that I may look more simply to him."

In personal self-control and humble submission to his Lord, Carey set out to continue his commitment to the people of India. "I trust the work will lose nothing of real value. We are not discouraged; indeed, the work is already begun again in every language. We are cast down but not in despair." By 1832 Carey's rebuilt and expanded printing operation had published complete Bible or portions of the Bible in forty-four languages and dialects.[4]

What does Jesus want me to know?

Why does He want me to know this?

What does He want me to do in response?

Day Four

"Blessed are those who hunger and thirst after
righteousness for they will be satisfied."

MATTHEW 5:6

The meaning of anything depends on what one initially brings to it. This beatitude is difficult for those of us who live in western civilization to appreciate or understand, especially in the twenty-first century. Hungry? Thirsty? Us? Superabundance is all around us. Not so in Jesus' day nor in many parts of the world today.

Those hearing the teaching of Jesus lived hand-to-mouth. They were forever on the brink of starvation, and good drinking water was hard to find. Life was cruel. The hunger and thirst of the day was no genteel matter. It was literally a matter of life or death. Jesus was not speaking to people who had pantries filled with groceries and were snacking on chips and sipping a soft drink.

The concept underlying Jesus teaches in this beatitude is: How much do you want to be righteous? How important is it to you? Do you passionately seek to be like Jesus, righteous in all of your ways and dealings? Is your desire to be righteous so compelling that you would be like the starving man dumpster-diving to find a scrap of bread? Or is righteousness a passing curiosity that might pause momentarily in our mind during a sermon and then dissipate? It seems a bit extreme doesn't it?

The issue of righteousness (right standing with God) has its root in one coming to grasp his natural condition before God. As we saw in the first beatitude, only when one accepts that there is absolutely nothing they can do to establish their rightness with God can they find a basis for becoming righteousness. Everyone is naturally and eternally separated from God because they were born with a fatal (spiritual) defect. The only hope is to receive the gift God offers. But it is costly in that one has to surrender their life to Jesus to receive it. How humbling! How much do you want eternal life? There is only one alternative—hell. Yet, it is a universal deception that a person may earn a right standing with God by what they do. It's a reasonable concept, but it is eternally destructive.

The issue in our time seems to be that we want just enough righteousness to satisfy the moment, and then we move on to more important stuff like watching TV, shopping, or social media. The issue this beatitude presents is that it is quite demanding and daunting while (at the same time) promising the most satisfaction.

It is fascinating to note that there is a spark of goodness even in people who seem to be completely depraved. A ruthless murderer befriends an abandoned kitten. A ruthless tycoon secretly gives money to a hospital for children. Somehow, there is still a dim reflection of the Creator in the worst of humankind. Unfortunately, that spark of goodness doesn't find its way to becoming a full blaze because, "Honestly, I just don't want to make righteousness the centerpiece of my life. It's just too much."

All these previous thoughts on the subject come into focus when Greek grammar is applied. In the verb tenses of this beatitude, the essence of hungering and thirsting for righteousness emerges. The difference between the partial and the whole becomes relevant. One person may desire a slice of bread; another may desire the whole loaf. The verb tense determines if a person is saying, "I want a swallow of water" or "I want the whole pitcher of water."

Jesus said, "Blessed is the person who wants the whole loaf, the whole pitcher of righteousness." Whatever it takes, I want it all—nothing left out. That person will know the blessed satisfaction far surpassing anything else one can experience in life. Since "righteousness" is so valuable, we need to be sure we understand what it is.

As Jesus taught it, righteousness is the state of being consistent with the character of God—those qualities of "right-ness" which God defines. All of those character qualities found in God (perhaps summarized in the Ten Commandments). God says that each of the Ten Commandments is right. The Christian who hungers and thirsts for righteousness will develop a lifestyle of living out what is right, as God defines "right."

"Blessed is the person who so passionately seeks to display the character of God that nothing gets in the way of that becoming a reality. Such persons will find true satisfaction and contentment."

The Messenger Needed The Message

It might surprise you to learn that one of the best-known men in Christian history, the "father" of the Methodist faith, was one of those who built his hope of eternal life on the understanding that he had to earn it, deserve it, to be righteous. His righteousness was self-righteousness.

In 1735, John Wesley and a few others sailed to America as missionaries to the colony of Georgia. During the voyage, a storm left John cowering in fear of death. He was scared nearly to death and was amazed to observe the Moravians on board who seemed to have something he did not have. Upon landing in Georgia, he plunged into missionary work. He was totally sincere, but his efforts were unsatisfactory.

It became clear to Wesley that the very message he was preaching to the Indians was a message in which he did not have confidence. With incredible honesty, he admitted he could talk about his belief in the gospel when there was no threat or pressure. But, when confronted—as he was at times—with a life-threatening situation, he lost his confidence that death would be gain.

A short time after that, John returned to England. There he came under the influence of Peter Boehler, a Moravian. Through him, John was introduced to the writings of Martin Luther, especially Luther's commentaries on Galatians and Romans. The realization came crystal clear: he had been depending on his works, not faith. His theology was sinking sand. This realization was clear in his mind, but it was not yet in his heart.

John's brother, Charles, struggled with the same theological problem. During a time when Charles was quite ill, John and others prayed for his healing and prayed that all of them might gain the assurance of salvation. Charles got it. He surrendered to Christ with great rejoicing. Not so with John. For three days, he struggled night and day. He found no peace. Never was one more consumed with being right with God.

The outcome of this struggle came about in a simple but extraordinary way. John often shared what brought about the change. One evening, he was walking down Aldersgate Street distracted by his misery and in no mood to go to church. He heard what sounded like a religious service in progress. Reluctantly, he joined the small group where a man was reading Luther's preface to the Epistle to the Romans. About a quarter before nine o'clock—he related in many sermons after that–he felt his heart "strangely warmed." Suddenly, the message became clear, and he felt Christ alone was his hope for salvation. He realized Christ had taken away his sins and saved him at that same time. John preached salvation by grace through faith in Jesus Christ nonstop thereafter until he died in 1791.[5]

What does Jesus want me to know?

Why does He want me to know this?

What does He want me to do in response?

Day Five

"Blessed are the merciful for they shall obtain mercy."

MATTHEW 5:7

As stated before, Jesus spoke in Aramaic, joining meanings from both the Greek and Hebrew languages. When we understand Aramaic, the meaning of the beatitudes is made clear. The Greek word for "mercy" is *eleemon*. The Hebrew word for "mercy" *chesedh*. The Aramaic brings in the meaning of both. Jesus is saying that the merciful are not those who are just sympathetic (I-am-so-sorry-you-are-going-through-this). Such sympathy is good, but it is only surface. It is a sad, external acknowledgment, but that is its extent. Not so with the truly merciful.

The merciful see, feel, and think about what another is experiencing. They step to the person's side who is in pain, sorrow, or need and walk with them through the difficulty. This is a deliberate, time-consuming commitment. The merciful are perceptive, empathetic, and willing to sweat right alongside the in need. The quality of mercy is very clear in an incident near the time of the crucifixion. Jesus desperately needed a time of quiet and rest, a time of reflection. He turned aside from grueling ministry and stopped at the home of

Mary, Martha, and Lazarus as He had done so often. He knew that His days were limited.

Martha was sympathetic and busied herself with getting a meal ready for her dear friend, knowing something of the demands He had been through. She was a true friend, sympathetic and serving. Her efforts were completely unselfish and commendable. She was giving Him the best she had to offer as an expression of her love and devotion. But she missed the point. Mary got it. She perceived what Jesus was thinking and feeling and what He was seeking—at least in part. Sitting quietly with Him. She offered her companionship. Mercy.

The merciful have matured to the place where they pay attention. They have come to understand that each person thinks and acts the way they do for a reason. The merciful don't react to the negativity of another; they respond to it. They deliberately seek to understand and work with the person. The merciful desire to see through the sufferer's eyes and feel what they feel.

It is said that when Queen Victoria learned that a dear friend had lost her husband at almost the same time the queen's husband died, she quietly went to her friend's home. When the friend attempted to stand and acknowledge the Queen, Queen Victoria quickly assured her that she was not to rise because the queen had arrived. She had only come as one woman to another. It was a touching gesture, expressing the pain of losing a husband.

Surely that is what our Father did in Jesus. Jesus came to live inside our skin while we endure the challenges of life. He thinks with us. He sees what we see; He feels what we feel. Our weaknesses touch Him. So much so that He died for us. He is an ever-present and involved Merciful One in our times of trouble.

"How blessed are those who care enough to get involved...to get inside another person and see, feel, and think as they do...who go through it all with them. Those are the merciful, and they will find that others will do the same for them."

What does Jesus want me to know?

Why does He want me to know this?

What does He want me to do in response?

Day Six

"Blessed are the pure in heart for they shall see God."

MATTHEW 5:8

These beatitudes are tremendously challenging, aren't they?! As noted before, each of the beatitudes is simple in wording, but they carry enormous, eternal impact. None of the beatitudes are more challenging than this one. Two thoughts dominate this beatitude: motive and extent.

The Greek word *katharos* hits us like a sledgehammer in its various shades of meaning. First, it means to be clean. Soiled, sweaty work clothes are thoroughly washed, so they become clean. To be pure is to be clean, inside and out, entirely. Imagine the filthiest clothes made as white as snow as clean as they can be.

The second meaning of pure is illustrated in a common practice on the farm. Grain was threshed and collected into baskets. These baskets were then taken to an elevation and poured from one basket to another as the breeze blew away the chaff. With the debris gone, the grain that remained in the second basket was pure and was ready for use.

A final meaning of pure comes from a related word to *katharos*. It is *akeratos*. It speaks of pure milk; no water has been added. The milk is unadulterated, undiluted. The same illustration applies to wine or to metal that has been purified of all the dross by fire. Pure means clean, cleansed of impurity, undiluted, uncontaminated, unalloyed, free from any mixture of any impurity.

With this beatitude, Jesus was teaching that the pure person is first free from any selfish motive. Since God looks on the heart (the intent) first—this is a challenge indeed. Who can say that the deeds are done are unmixed in motive? As commendable as it is to do the right deed secretly—the left hand not knowing what the right hand is doing—who does that? Other people may never know such secret acts, but God does. Do we find that there is a sense of self-congratulation, self-serving in such deeds deep down? Is it not true after the secret deed has been done, that deep down, we hope that somehow what we have done will be made known?

Is it not true that, while we publicly present ourselves as not wanting the spotlight, we secretly do? Is it not true that we outwardly resist our name being called and attached to some noble deed, that we are inwardly irritated when it is not revealed? To be pure in heart, is it not here that our greatest struggle with hypocrisy begins?

Can any of us say that we have unmixed, unalloyed pure motives as a way of life? This beatitude demands the most exacting self-examination. To honestly, purely examine our motives is extremely difficult and shaming.

Why does it matter that we pure in heart (notice the "heart") ...and not just in the public view? Because the heart is the true us. Because only those who have an uncontaminated, unobstructed (in act and motive) purity get to see God as He really is. It is a fact that we can see only what we can see. We all have seen those pictures or drawings in which more than one image is presented. Two images are present at the same time. Can you "see" both images? Other images consist of a chart with numbers or letters, all the same except for one number or letter. Can you see the different letters or numbers? Drafting technicians can see an angle. The craftsman remodeling a home can "see" the finished project. Some can see; some cannot.

Some people are so depraved that they only see the filthy or degrading. They comment on the most innocent conversation turning it into something hateful, negative, or dirty. Jesus said in Matthew 12:34 "...out of the abundance of the heart, the mouth speaks." What is in the heart will eventually surface.

When one is pure in heart, one can see God in His creation. They can see true goodness that others miss completely. They can see God as the pastor expounds the Scripture. They can see the agony and the glory of the cross and the empty tomb. It is God they see and not some cheap, obstructed, distorted caricature. Oh, the blessedness of the person whose motives are unadulterated, and whose view is unobstructed from here to eternity...for they shall see God as He is.

Grateful for Blindness!?

Interestingly enough, multitudes in the Christian faith have been able to see God through some who where were totally blind. One such blind saint was Fanny Crosby who "saw" God in a marvelous way. She was born in 1820 and when she was six weeks old, she caught a cold that inflamed her eyes. Her parents called for a doctor but the man who came—presenting himself as a doctor—recommended a poultice for her eyes which resulted in Fanny's blindness. The "doctor" disappeared and was never heard from again. Fanny's father died when she was one year old.

Learning of Fanny's blindness, her grandmother said, "Then I will be her eyes." She spent hours and hours describing flowers, sunsets, bumble bees, etc. When Fanny was nine years of age, another influential person entered her life, a Mrs. Hawley, who taught her poetry and the Bible. By the age of ten, Fanny had memorized whole books of the Bible.

At age fifteen, she entered the Institute for the Blind in New York City and studied there for seven years, later returning to teach there for eleven years. She had a phenomenal memory and used that memory rather than braille to record poetry. She was quite gifted in composing and editing poetry in her head.

In the fall of 1850, Fanny and some of her friends began attending revival services at the Thirtieth Street Methodist Church in New York. She responded to the invitation twice but found no real peace. Then on November 20, 1850, while the choir sang *"Alas and Did My Savior Bleed."* When the choir reached the last verse, "Here Lord, I give myself away," Fanny was filled with joy unspeakable and full of glory. She "saw" the Savior and gave herself to Him. Eleven years later, she began writing hymns.

Fanny met and married a fellow Institute for the Blind student, Alexander van Alstyne. She was thirty-eight, and she kept her maiden name. They had one child who died in infancy. She became one of the most prolific writers in history, writing over 9,000 hymns before her death in 1915. Approximately sixty of her hymns are still in popular use including, "Blessed Assurance" "Rescue the Perishing,"

"Praise Him, Praise Him," "To God Be the Glory," "Pass Me Not," "Jesus Keep Me Near the Cross" and many others.

This one whose blind eyes were opened to see the Blessed Savior in verse, was a frequent guest at the White House. She traveled throughout the world and had a multitude of famous friends. She was never shy about sharing the gospel. She also never wanted sympathy because of her blindness. Asked if she ever regretted not being able to see, she responded, "If I had been given a choice at birth, I would have asked to be blind...for when I get to heaven, the first face I will see will be the One who died for me."[6]

What does Jesus want me to know?

Why does He want me to know this?

What does He want me to do in response?

Day Seven

"Blessed are the peacemakers for they shall be called the sons of God."

MATTHEW 5:9

Some people are never happy unless they are stirring up trouble. They seem to always be on the lookout for conflict. Why? It is hard to say. Perhaps they are so stunted and damaged in self-esteem that getting involved in trouble is the only way to get noticed. Most people prefer peace, sometimes peace at any price. That is not what Jesus said. Jesus was all about peace. He is called the Prince of Peace. That's why He came: to bring peace instead of insurrection. But He came to be a peace-MAKER. His primary purpose was not to be a peacekeeper, for there was little peace to be found. He came to be a peacemaker. Peace at any price is no peace at all. Peace requires action.

Some so fear trouble or conflict that they either ignore it or go out of their way to avoid it. This is understandable, but the trouble/conflict continues unless someone takes the initiative to make peace. Blessed are the ones who take the initiative to make the world a better place to live. Wrong, injustice, and trouble must be confronted in the right way and at the right time if one is to live by this beatitude.

Neither the Greek word *eirene* nor the Hebrew word *shalom* mean the <u>absence</u> of trouble. These words mean that, but they mean so much more. Peace is not the absence of trouble because that just creates a vacuum. Peace fills the void with the <u>presence</u> of everything good for a person. Peace-lovers may avoid trouble, but that is not always good for them or the conflicted. Making peace eliminates the trouble <u>and</u> solidifies all things good for the parties.

Blessed is the one who takes the initiative to defeat trouble and create good in every way. Such a person is directly involved in the work of God (Romans 5:33; II Corinthians 13:11; Hebrews 13:20). To paraphrase President Lincoln, "Whenever I have the opportunity, I always try to pull a weed and plant a flower in its place." Such a commitment to peacemaking comes after every person's inner civil war is settled. The civil war is waged between my way and God's way; His will or my will. To surrender to the Prince of Peace positions one to become a peacemaker.

Perhaps the crowning meaning of this beatitude is to focus on the very work God is committed to—reconciling the un-reconciled. No conflict can ultimately be resolved until there is peace with God through the finished work of Jesus. The outward conflict between two parties is only the symptom of the actual conflict.

"Blessed is the person who (appropriately) will not stop with the outward conflict but makes every effort to bring the conflicted ones to Jesus."

From the Boardroom to the Laundry Room

One of the most unlikely candidates to illustrate this beatitude was a hard-boiled former Marine. A senior partner in a prestigious law firm in Washington D. C., Chuck Colson received a stunning phone call in 1969. Known in the media as President Nixon's hatchet man, Chuck Colson was recruited to handle the President's dirty work. Then Watergate came. Before long, indictments followed, and Colson resigned his position at the White House and formed his law firm.

Before visiting a former client, Tom Phillips, in March 1973, Colson was told that Phillips had become involved in religion. During the visit, the subject came up, and Colson was stunned when Phillips told him what he had heard was true. He had accepted Christ, and it was the most marvelous experience of his life. Colson hastened to change the subject.

As the visit ended, Phillips walked Colson to the door and suggested that he would like to tell Colson the whole story of his experience with Christ. He shared that he was to the point that life was not worth living before Christ changed him. The part about life not being worth living struck a raw nerve with Colson.

While on vacation in the summer of 1973, Chuck called Phillips, who invited him to his home. Colson went. Phillips gave it to him straight. Referencing a book, *Mere Christianity*, by C. S. Lewis, Phillips described pride as a cancer that prevents a person from knowing God. It hit Colson hard, and as he left, Phillips gave him a copy of the book.

Sitting in his car on the night of August 12, 1973, Colson later related that he began to weep uncontrollably. All he could say was, "Take me! Take me!" His heart was there, but his brilliant mind had not grasped the message yet. He poured over *Mere Christianity*. A short time later, with understanding, he prayed, "Lord Jesus, I believe you. I accept you. Please come into my life. I commit it to you."

Shortly after that, Colson learned of a prayer group led by Democratic Senator Harold Hughes. He became a part. With the support of these new brothers, he decided to plead guilty to a Watergate crime for which he had not been charged. He was sentenced to prison for from one to three years. The new prisoner in charge of the laundry at Maxwell Federal Prison was formerly special counsel to the president of the United States: Charles Colson. By the end of seven months, his family was falling apart. His wife was near the breaking point; a son was in prison for narcotics possession. He was released.

In 1976, Chuck Colson founded Prison Fellowship, a worldwide ministry to those who have no peace. Hundreds of prisons in most of the countries of the world now have the presence of peacemakers daily seeking to bring peace to the most desperate men and women in the world.[7]

What does Jesus want me to know?

Why does He want me to know this?

What does He want me to do in response?

Day Eight

"Blessed are those who are persecuted for righteousness'
sake, for theirs is the kingdom of heaven. Blessed are you
when they revile and persecute you, and say all kinds of evil
against you falsely for my sake. Rejoice and be exceedingly
glad, for great is your reward in heaven, for so they
persecuted the prophets who were before you."

MATTHEW 5:10-12

One thing that accounts for the shallowness of Christianity today is the truth contained in these three verses. In their zeal to see people reconciled to God, evangelical Christians too often ignore a fundamental and indispensable fact: to become a Christian will cost you. It will cost you your life. To become a Christian means, you are not your own anymore. You are bought and paid for. Someone Else has the "say." Far too often the earnest, but unwise "soul winner" will say, "All you have to do is ask Jesus into your heart." The implication is that becoming a Christian is easy, simple. It is, if you understand what you are doing, but the simple is not simplistic. Becoming a Christian is not complicated but it is profound in its effect.

The salvation of the soul of a person costs God everything. It costs the same for the Christian. So if you are hearing the gospel as it is, consider carefully what you are getting into before you "sign up." It is eternally criminal to fail to make the cost of salvation clear when presenting the gospel. The necessity for repentance (Jesus said, "Unless you repent...you will perish.") is often glossed over. You cannot belong to and go on with God and remain as you are. Salvation is not turning over a new leaf, cleaning up your act, or giving your sins to God. Salvation involves God's first desire: you.

There is a remarkable similarity between the first and twenty-first centuries. One similarity is seen in the Christian community. In the first century and (in third world countries today, particularly Muslim-dominated countries), becoming a Christian affected every area of your life. It is not uncommon today for one living in one of these countries to be considered dead by their family when they commit to Christ. Funeral services are held for those who have departed from their ancestral faith to become Christians.

In the first century and those third world countries today, every dimension of life was affected: employment, family, social, etc. Fundamental decisions must be considered if one becomes a Christian. Examples: If I am employed in a God-dishonoring job, do I stay? Does a special relationship with a member of the other sex require me to violate Christian convictions? Are there certain habits that I must abandon? It costs to be an actual (not cultural) Christian.

Though many would consider such a serious approach to becoming a Christian to be legalism, Jesus meant the Sermon on the Mount to be taken literally. To cultural Christianity, the Christian life (as the Bible defines normal) is so contradictory to what is culturally accepted that "Christian" is considered abnormal. For example, cultural Christianity takes the position: "One has to live, so the source of employment is irrelevant." The faithful Christian listens carefully to God and His word and responds, "Really?" The Bible says "Yes, and all who desire to live godly in Christ Jesus WILL suffer persecution." (II Timothy 3:12, emphasis added).

Persecution may take the form of ridicule, mocking, harassment, imprisonment, even physical torture. But it also takes the form of leveraging one away from true Christianity. Persecution may have social aspects. As mentioned, one's own family might disown them. A non-Christian marriage partner may walk away. Feasts in honor of pagan gods were common social gatherings, and the Christians were not welcome, nor could they participate anyway.

Persecution for the crime of being a Christian might have physical implications. To stand on Christian principles might well result in arrest and imprisonment. In the first century, Christians were thrown into the arena to entertain the crowds at pagan games. The crowds were entertained as wild animals tore Christians apart. Some were burned alive at the stake or tortured to the point of an agonizing death.

Though Christians were by conviction the best employees an owner had, being more loyal, fruitful, and dependable than their pagan counterparts, they were often persecuted. Why? Moral convictions regarding honesty, purity, and unwillingness to cut corners made for a convicting environment. Christians, by their very character, brought resentment and persecution.

In the general culture, other things led to persecution as well. The pagan community heard many rumors about the Christians, and these rumors were widely spread and believed. Christian communion (the Lord's Supper) was widely reported as being cannibalistic. Christians ate a body and drank the blood of another, the pagans said. The love feasts were reported to be the grossest of immoral practices. The Christian belief that the world would end in flames was proof to the pagans that they were incendiaries and were part of a secret group set upon destroying the world, the pagans believed.

The Roman government had reasons for persecuting the Christians and the Christian religion. The Romans ruled a vast and varied empire. There were countless cultures and religions, and each of them was a potential source of insurrection. Rome needed a single system to bring all conquered peoples to a uniform loyalty. A basic religious demand was determined to be the answer. One unifying order was that all people proclaim their allegiance, to Caesar as Lord, confirmed by an oath. Once a person had sworn a commitment to Caesar as Lord, they could do as they pleased as long as they caused no trouble. Christians refused to make such an oath. They had one Lord—the Lord Jesus Christ. At the risk of their very lives, they held loyally to the Lord Jesus. Rome would not tolerate their disloyalty to Caesar. Official government persecution was the result.

Faithful Unto Death

Polycarp is a historical person. His pastor at Ephesus was the Apostle John from the Isle of Patmos. A short time after finishing the last book of the Bible, John returned to his beloved Ephesian congregation. Polycarp was a leader of the Ephesian church. His testimony at his trial for being a Christian exemplifies how deeply early Christians held their convictions. Polycarp (the Bishop of Smyrna) was was arranged before a Roman tribunal and confronted: Pledge your loyalty to Caesar or die. His immortal response was that he had served Christ eighty-six years, and Christ had never done him wrong. How could he now blaspheme his King who saved him? He would not recant, so they burned him at the stake. As the flames spread around his body, he expressed his gratitude that the Lord had considered him worthy to be burned at the stake because of his faith.

How strange and foolish such a conviction sounds to modern ears. Cultural Christianity considers persecution to be getting one's feelings hurt...not being invited to a social event...not having the pastor visit them in the hospital. To believe something so strongly as to die for it...deranged, crazy. Compromise is the first choice if the alternative is discomfort. At least, that is too often true in western Christianity. Thank God it is not true in many other parts of the world...and there, God is miraculously at work.

What further thought might we give to persecution? Why even consider the subject? Isn't it quite unlikely that persecution such as was experienced in the first century and third world countries will come to America? It is almost sure to come before Jesus comes again.

It would be wise to consider the following in the light of that probability.

1. To suffer persecution puts you in good company. The prophets and saints of old, together with modern-day martyrs, are our examples. Literally, we will tread where the saints have trod.

2. There may not be a more significant thing than deliberately making a decision that is more important than life itself. There are far worse things than dying for the Christian.

3. Jesus said when persecution comes as a result of standing on your convictions, you should (literally) "Leap for joy for great is your reward in heaven," (Matthew 5:12).

4. If need be, to die for one's faith is to continue the unbroken chain of honor and eternal conviction that Jesus lived and taught.

5. No person suffering persecution suffers alone. The invisible presence of those who were persecuted attends to the persecuted. Most of all, Jesus is there. Just as He was with the "three Hebrew children" in Daniel's day, so in a mysterious way, He will be with all who are persecuted.

To be sure, I do not want to be persecuted, really persecuted. I worry about the quality and durability of my faith if faced with life or death. It is easier to think of such things now that I have little life left anyway; still, it concerns me. Would I stand the test? There is some comfort in believing that grace sufficient for the need is provided at the time of the need...not before. Manna was provided each day. There was always enough, just enough, and any attempt to hoard rotted. So, the grace of God for each day and occasion will be enough. I want to believe that. I pray for succeeding generations.

When the great Hoover Dam was completed, a plaque was fixed to the wall in honor of those who died in the dam construction. The inscription reads, "These died that the desert might rejoice and blossom as a rose." May I be willing to endure persecution for others to escape the desert of separation from God.

When Death is Moments Away

Many of us remember the Rwanda genocide that occurred in 1964. No more explicit example of the reality of the cost of discipleship can be found than in the experience of a Tutsi pastor, Yona Kanamuzeyi, and his friend Andrew Kayumba. These two Christian brothers remind us of the reality of this text.

Pastor Yona had created a network of twenty-four village churches and ministered to over 6,000 each month. Being of the Tutsi tribe—the political leaders of Rwanda though a minority in population—Pastor Yona was one of the first to be rounded up by the Hutu rebellion, which overthrew the government. The Hutus—the majority of the population—vented their rage on the Tutsis who had ruled them for generations. International missionaries who brought Christianity to Rwanda were removed when political, violent turmoil escalated. The hope of the Christian community rested in the likes of Pastor Yona.

On January 24, 1964, a jeep pulled up to Pastor Yona's tent in the refugee camp. Hutu troops ordered the pastor and his friend Andrew into the jeep. Pastor Yona knew that death was certain for both him and his friend unless God intervened. In the military camp, Pastor Yona asked permission to write a note to his wife and pray. He prayed that God, who knew there were no legitimate charges against him and Andrew, would be merciful to those who would take their lives. The men were driven to a bridge over the river. The pastor was told to get out and as he walked away beside the soldiers, his friend Andrew heard him singing,

There's a land that is fairer than day
And by faith, we can see it afar

For the Father waits over the way
To prepare us a dwelling place there.[8]

The crack of a rifle shot silenced the song. The soldiers dumped Pastor Yona's body over the side of the bridge into the river below. Andrew was driven back to his tent with the stern warning, "If you tell anyone, you, too, will be killed." The pastor's note made it to his wife: "We are going to heaven."[9]

What does Jesus want me to know?

Why does He want me to know this?

What does He want me to do in response?

Day Nine

*"...you are the salt of the earth; but if the salt loses its flavor,
how shall it be seasoned? It is then good for nothing but to
be thrown out and trampled underfoot by men."*

MATTHEW 5:13

Those hearing this statement from Jesus must have looked around, astounded. Who is "you?" Surely you don't mean us, disciples. We are just common, ordinary men. We have no influence or clout. Nobody of importance knows us; we are just ordinary working-class people. Besides, we are living under occupation. Rome rules the earth. We... the salt of the earth?

In the ancient world, salt was a highly-prized commodity. The best salt came from the sea. Pools of water were transferred from the sea, and evaporation reduced the water to salt crystals. It was a long and tedious process. Salt was both literally and figuratively of great value. Away from the sea, there were "salt licks." These were natural seeping springs that were unusually salty. Animals from all around came to "lick" the salt that came from these springs. Some plants adapted to the salty conditions, and the plants themselves had a salty taste. These plants were gathered by natives in a laborious process and provided a measure of saltiness when rubbed on food or included in the cooking process. It was not the best, but it was better than nothing.

Salt had several benefits. Two benefits stand out: taste enhancement and preservation. This was the analogy Jesus was applying to His followers. You are to enhance your environment in godly ways, and you are a preserving influence where corruption is rampant. First, salt as a preservative was valuable because without it, food, especially meat, spoiled easily and quickly in the hot Palestinian sun. I grew up in an era when there was always a supply of "sugar cure" at hog-killing time, which was a spicy salt used on fresh meat. It was very effective. It drew out excess moisture from the meat and preserved it so that it remained tasty for months.

Christian, you exist in a decaying world; corruption is everywhere. Dishonesty, greed, immorality...every kind of moral and spiritual degradation is rampant. It is to such a world that Jesus deployed His disciples. In the same way, He commissioned us. Having "rubbed up against Jesus," the disciples had become "salty," at least to some degree. They would become saltier as they knew Him better. Now, He was sending them out to rub up against decaying humanity. The eternal destiny of souls depended upon it.

Who rubbed up against you and brought you to Jesus? Who cared enough to stay with you until you surrendered to Him? Who pulled you, a burning brand, from the fire? Who are you rubbing up against today?

Second, salt draws out the flavor in food. How bland food would be if there were no salt. Christians are to be for those who are perishing, a sweet savor creating a hunger for the Savior. It is tragic that so many Christians are negative, critical, pessimistic whiners. They look like they were weaned on a dill pickle and never got over it. Their motto is: "Don't worry, nothing is going to turn out right." Oliver Wendell Holmes is said to have remarked that he might have entered the ministry had not clergy members looked so much like undertakers.

Who in this world should be more joyful and spread that joy all around than the redeemed? Rescued from the power of sin, set upon a course of hope and assurance, how can a Christian be downcast? A gloomy Christian is a contradiction.

Negative, gloomy Christians are suitable only to thatch a roof or be used to "pave" a road. They neither preserve the good nor draw out the best. They have lost their usefulness as Christians have allowed the world to influence them rather than the other way around.

Yes, you ordinary working-class people are precious in God's plans for the ages. Remind yourselves who (and Whose) you are. Remind yourselves of what you bring to the circle you move in. Remind yourselves of the Jesus within you and all of the resources He provides. Now, get out there and rub up against those who need the real deal!

Betrayed

The Ten Boom family lived in Nazi-occupied Haarlem, Netherlands, in 1944. Father, Casper, repaired watches, assisted by his daughters, Corrie and Betsy. The family lived quietly above their business to not attract the attention of the Gestapo, but more importantly, because they had a secret: they hid Jewish people attempting to avoid the Holocaust.

A man with a broken watch appeared one morning and quietly mentioned his family was hiding Jews. His wife had just been arrested. Could they help? Believing God had called them to aid the Jews, Corrie agreed. The stranger left. That night, the Gestapo crashed down their door and arrested the family.

Along with the Ten Boom's, thirty-three others in their network were arrested and beaten for hiding Jews. Despite two days of searching, the Gestapo did not find six Jews hiding behind a false wall in a bedroom. They ultimately survived.

The family was shipped to the Ravensbruck concentration camp. Ten days later, Casper died. Later, while in Ravensbruck, Betsy died as well on Christmas Day. Corrie survived, and many of us know her through the book *The Hiding Place* and the movie made of her life. I ask myself, "Am I salt...?"[10]

What does Jesus want me to know?

Why does He want me to know this?

What does He want me to do in response?

Day Ten

*"You are the light of the world. A city that is set on a hill
cannot be hidden. Nor do they light a lamp and put it
under a basket, but on a lampstand, and it gives light to
all who are in the house. Let your light so shine before men
that they may see your good works and glorify your Father
in heaven."*

MATTHEW 5:14-15

Jesus came to be who we are so that we might become who He is.
In every way (except for sin), Jesus was just like us while at the same
time being God. He is the Light of the world. That is what we are.
What did Jesus mean by this second identity He gave His disciples?

1. Light reveals. It shows what is. It reveals the path forward.
    The Christian is (with the mind and spirit of Christ) the one
    to reveal a wrong being anticipated or done. They stand and
    indicate what is wrong and shows the right way forward. The
    Christian is the light for others to follow.

2. Light is seen; it has no purpose otherwise. There is clarity in
    the light; there is no clarity in invisible light. In Jesus' day,
    when a family left home, they placed a vessel over the light

source in the house. That light source was a wick extending from a "gravy boat" spout that contained olive oil. A wick was challenging to light in the day before matches.

3. A clay vessel was placed over it to keep the light burning and prevent its accidentally setting fire to the home. Remove the covering, light the house...that's why it existed. True for Christians; we exist to display Jesus.

4. Light guides. Lights reveal the runway at the airport for an approaching aircraft—lights guide traffic along thoroughfares, especially dangerous intersections. The light shines forth from the lighthouse, warning of danger. Christian, you are in the world at large to show the way. Warn of danger, assure the uncertain, be a beacon of hope and trust in an insecure world.

5. Light is derived. Scientists have a term for derived or reflected light. The term is *albedo*: the measurement of how much light is reflected from a celestial body. The planet Venus reflects the greatest amount of light, .65 or 65% of the light which strikes its surface. Our moon reflects only 7% of the sunlight which crosses it. The sun is the source; the celestial bodies reflect the light. Jesus applied His point. When Jesus comes inside us at the new birth, He is the source of the light that shines out in our attitude and action. We are not the source; we reflect the source. *Alos* is the word for "good." It means that a thing is not only a good thing but also attractive and winsome at the same time. Christian goodness is a joy to behold.

Even when good deeds involve correction or rebuke, it acts with compassion, with an arm around the shoulders. Good deeds are to be done. They are to be seen...but not selfishly. The good deed is done to display and draw attention to God—to reflect His character. Good deeds done to be seen of men have their reward then and there, and the reward is only from men. Such acts have zero eternal benefits or rewards.

Faithful to the Last Breath

We remember that John Wesley had difficulty accepting that right standing with God was by grace through faith in Christ alone. Desperately seeking to know God, he found it near-impossible to surrender in simple faith and receive the gift purchased for him at Calvary. On that cold night when he "...found himself strangely warmed..." by the message from Luther's Preface to the Book of Romans, he surrendered. A fire was lit that blazed against all odds and discomforts for the rest of his life.

Nearing the end of his days, at age 87 and in failing health, he had continued to preach regularly in the open air as he had done so effectively for many years. On February 23, 1791, Wesley received a plea from a wealthy London merchant whom he hardly knew. Mr. Belson had lost his wife and badly needed the counsel of a godly man. Wesley made the sixteen-mile trek to the Belson home and counseled the grieving man for an hour and a half.

As Wesley prepared to go home, weary and not feeling well, Mr. Belson informed him that he had sent his servants into the village, inviting the community to come and hear a message from Wesley. A crowd overflowed the Belson home, and Wesley spoke from Isaiah 55:6: "Seek ye the Lord while He may be found..." It was his last sermon. It had been a long Wednesday.

The next day, an assistant shared a tract written by an African slave who found his freedom and became a Christian. Wesley was so moved by the message that he dictated a letter to his friend William Wilberforce, the leading opposition to the slave trade in Parliament. This was Wesley's last correspondence with Wilberforce.

He pleaded with him not to grow weary in well-doing and to sustain the fight against slavery, especially in America. The following Wednesday, March 2, 1791, with friends and family kneeling beside his bed, he said his final word on earth, "Farewell." Their sadness was diminished by the knowledge that he and entered the joy of the Lord. Let your light shine to the last breath![11]

What does Jesus want me to know?

Why does He want me to know this?

What does He want me to do in response?

Day Eleven

"Do not think that I came to destroy the Law or the Prophets. I did not come to destroy but to fulfill. For assuredly, I say to you, till heaven and earth pass away, one jot or one tittle will by no means pass from the law till all is fulfilled. Whoever therefore breaks one of the least of these commandments and teaches men so, shall be called least in the kingdom of heaven; but whoever does and teaches them, he shall be called great in the kingdom of heaven. For I say to you, that unless our righteousness exceeds the righteousness of the scribes and Pharisees, you will by no means enter the kingdom of heaven."

MATTHEW 5:17-20

At first reading, this seems to be a strange, contradictory passage. Did not Jesus violate the law on many occasions? Did He not heal people on the Sabbath? Did He not eat without first washing His hands? Was not He crucified because He was a lawbreaker? Yes. How is it then that He is the end of the law as Paul said in Romans 10:4 while at the same time He lays down the eternal character of the law? We can understand what Jesus said by defining the terms in His statement. When the Jews spoke of "the law," they did so in one of four ways:

1. The Ten Commandments
2. The first five books of the Bible
3. The law and the Prophets, that is, the Old Testament
4. The oral and scribal law

The meaning of "the law" in the days of Jesus was most commonly the oral and scribal law. It is this law that Jesus and Paul condemned. In the Ten Commandments, there are no rules at all, just ten great, timeless principles. When they were given to Moses, they stood pristine, written in simple and easily understood words. The instruction was just to obey them. Nothing more was needed.

In time, the Jewish elite thought the simple Ten Commandments were not enough. Since the Commandments were God's foundational standard, they reasoned that one could not risk simple obedience. The elite reasoned that the meaning must be implied if not explicitly stated because God addresses every situation in life. If not explicitly stated, then the implication must be determined to gain a right standing with God.

Who was to decide? What needed to be added to the Commandments so that the ordinary Jew could comply? Of course, the scribes were just the ones for the task! This group of men set out to define and address every conceivable human circumstance so that compliance with the law could be determined. Tens of thousands of rules and regulations resulted.

An example of such scribal work relates to the Sabbath. What did the commandment mean that no work was to be done on the Sabbath? First, the scribes had to determine a definition of "work." With much debate and hair-splitting, the scribes decided that work was "food equal to a dried fig, enough wine for mixing in a goblet, honey enough to put on a wound, enough water to moisten an eye-salve or to write two letters of the alphabet" ...and on and on, endlessly.

Might a tailor violate the Sabbath if he forgot and left a needle in a garment and the owner wore the garment on the Sabbath, thus carrying a weight? Might a woman be in violation for wearing a pin or broach in her hair? Might a man be in violation if he lifted his child on the Sabbath? Might a person write two letters of the alphabet if he used permanent ink and then write additional letters with non-permanent ink like fruit juice or dust? Would that violate the Sabbath? Might a person respond to a person in danger of death? "Yes," the scribes said but only to stabilize the person and not let them get worse. A person could do nothing to make the person better.

The rules and regulations were endless, and the Pharisees (the separated ones) did little else but study and apply the laws, rules, and regulations the scribes developed. It also confirmed that some regulations were changed, and new applications had to be developed. At first, these scribal regulations were not written but oral. Generations of scribes memorized the regulations and carefully passed them on to succeeding generations. (The whole "institution" of scribes came about because it is estimated that not more than ten to twenty percent of the population was literate, so a group who could write was formalized with an official identity.)

These regulations were first summarized and codified about the middle of the third century AD. This summary was called the MISHNAH, and it made up a book of almost eight hundred pages (in English). Later, scribes wrote commentaries on the MISHNAH, known as the TALMUD. The Jerusalem TALMUD consisted of twelve volumes, the Babylonia, sixty volumes.

In the days of Jesus, Orthodox Jews believed serving God meant knowing and obeying these thousands of petty rules. Keeping these regulations was a matter of life or death and eternal destiny. It was this "law" that Jesus violated. This contradictory hodge-podge of legalistic foolishness was swept away, and the focus returned to the simple, unadorned law of God's original law. That law, Jesus honored.

The law of God, as Jesus defined it, is to be understood and obeyed. This is what He is teaching in the Sermon on the Mount. The law of God is not to be destroyed; it is timeless. It was the scribal law the Pharisees so relentlessly demanded obedience to that Jesus came to destroy. God's will cannot be found in the opaque morass of scribal law and interpretations.

The Ten Commandments still stand. In understanding and respecting them, there is the basis of reverence for God and man. Reverence for the principles of the Ten Commandments is the foundation for all law. Inscriptions in our own Supreme Court building in Washington D.C. affirm this. Other references to these Commandments are standards in the founding documents of our Republic.

In Jesus' teachings in three chapters in Matthew's gospel, we have the continuance from the past into the present. There had to be a law before the gospel could come. Without law, there can be no violation. God gave a law, and man violated it...reconciliation was necessary. Jesus saves only one kind of person—the lost. Until a person recognizes and acknowledges he is a sinner (he has missed the mark, fallen short) he is helpless to remedy his condition. He cannot save himself. When he does recognize he is a sinner and repents—asking God's mercy and grace, Jesus saves him. The law is necessary–God's law, not a man-made version.

Jesus is clear in brushing aside the man manuufactured law, but He is equally clear to say that honoring the law of God is not easy. God's law's responsibilities and duties are indeed demanding. The righteousness of the believer must EXCEED the righteousness of the Pharisees. This "exceeding" principle that Jesus developed in the Sermon on the Mount.

The Pharisees kept the law codified in the Mishna and the Talmud. Theoretically, one could adhere to the specifics of the law as the orthodox Jews defined it, but Jesus introduced a profound truth: *WHAT* a person does is of great importance, but the more significant issue is the *MOTIVE* one has for what he does.

The Pharisees did what they did for the sole purpose of gaining the approval of God by obedience to the law. The reality Jesus set forth was that love for God and man was the reason for obedience. Do what you do, motivated by love for God and your neighbor, not in a calculated adherence to rules and regulations which the scribes dreamed up.

> *"Were the whole realm of nature mine*
> *That were a present far too small,*
> *Love so amazing, so divine*
> *Demands my life, my heart, my all."[12]*

A King with Hidden Motives

There is no evidence King James of England was a particularly righteous man. Seeking some self-glory, but primarily to solidify his newly bestowed title of King in England as well as King of Scotland, He provides us fascinating evidence that Jesus meant exactly what He said in this text. A little history: When she died on March 24,

1603, Queen Elizabeth had ruled over England for forty-five years. She had neither husband nor children; she was married to England. Her wedding ring had to be filed from her finger. The Queen and England, inseparable.

While mourning her death, the nation learned that James VI, King of Scotland, would now become King James I, King of England as well. This was considered good news by the Church of England, which was laboring to free itself from Catholicism, the state church. The Puritans were hopeful as well. Wishing to show his willingness to listen to the petitions of these groups, King James convened the Hampton Court Conference on January 14, 1604. Somewhat full of himself, he opened the conference with his five-hour critique of the corruptions of the Church of England. The following day, he heard the petitions of the Puritans and promptly dismissed them. He focused, instead, on developing uniformity within his kingdom to solidify his control. Of all things, he sought to use a Bible to achieve his goal

He authorized the creation of what came to be called the King James Bible. Again, he did not do so because of his love for God or His kingdom. He needed a tool to stabilize and solidify his control over the Church of England. His subjects would unite through access to the Scriptures. He approved a list of fifty-four scholars; all but one were members of the Church of England. These middle-aged scholars were divided into six teams and met separately at Oxford, Westminster, and Cambridge. They were chosen for their skill in the ancient languages of the Bible, knowledge of theology, and biblical scholarship.

Drawing upon every resource available, the translating teams spent two years and nine months creating the most accurate translation they could produce. Some revisions were made later, but the translation was considered so accurate and reliable that it was not significantly revised for almost three hundred years when the Revised Standard Version was completed in 1885. For three hundred years, virtually every English-speaking family in the world had a King James Bible. Through its pages, millions came to know Jesus Christ personally. It is the single best-selling book of all time.

What does Jesus want me to know?

Why does He want me to know this?

What does He want me to do in response?

Day Twelve

"You have heard that it was said of those of old, 'You shall not murder, and whoever murders will be in danger of the judgment. But I say to you that whoever is angry with his brother without a cause shall be in danger of the judgment. And whoever says to his brother 'Raca!" shall be in danger of the council. But whoever says, 'You fool!' shall be in danger of hell fire."

MATTHEW 5:21-22

Jesus spoke with authority, original authority (Mark 1:22). Everything He said in Matthew 5-7 astonished His hearers (7:28-29). His authority was His own, affirmed by the Father, not in the authority the scribes found in the teachings of Rabbi __ or Rabbi __.

The Jewish rabbis of Jesus' day taught based on rules and regulations the scribes had added. They taught that those who deny that the law is from heaven have no part in the world to come. To this, Jesus responded by quoting the rabbis' law and then contradicted it four times.

He didn't argue or seek to prove his point. He calmly stated the truth on His authority. The prophet's authority came from the Lord (not I). The rabbi's cited previous scholars and used their statements as authoritative. Jesus said, "You have heard it said, but I say to you…" (Matthew 5:21, 27, 33, 38, 43) No wonder they were astonished. Not only did He dare to deny the entire law of the day flatly, but He also stated His law, and He did so with such authenticity and power that it was undeniable.

Jesus took the most incredible compilation of religious thought ever devised and corrected it. The summary of His correction is Matthew 5-7. Here is an amazing body of instruction—unheard of, revolutionary, and transforming. In a nutshell, Jesus said thoughts (motives) are just as important as deeds. It is not enough to avoid sinning; it is only enough when one has no desire or motivation to sin.

Every Christian is a walking civil war. The outward can be seen while there is the inward motivation that cannot be seen. Who can know the inward thoughts and motivations but the person alone… and God? None. It is, therefore, confirmed that only God has the right to judge. Nothing is hidden from Him, and to be angry with our brother without a cause (though it may be hidden away in the heart) is to be a murderer at heart. To lust for one (other than one's spouse) to have sexual relations with them (though that person may never know it) is a sin, just as is the actual act. Every person stands condemned, never able to defeat this imperfection. That is why Jesus came—to deal with both the outward and inward sin of every human being. Now, more detail.

The original commandment was "Thou shalt not commit murder." The commandment was not meant to apply to times of war or to capital punishment. The meaning, as Jesus clarified, is seen in the word *orge*. This is one of two words in Greek for anger. *Thumos* is anger that flashes, flares up quickly, and quickly subsides. It is different from *orge* as a quick grass fire from a long-continuing smoldering fire deep in a coal mine.

Orge is long-held, brooding anger that refuses to be extinguished. One who holds this kind of anger toward another, wishing him dead, is a murderer at heart. The actual act of murder is based on such anger and is held in check only by the fear of being caught and executed.

It is imperative to note that *orge* has both a negative and a positive side. Jesus is talking about the negative side. Though many modern translations delete "without a cause" from the King James text, I believe it should be included in the text. Anger for a just cause is legitimate, indeed, required. *Orge* is the word used for what motivated Jesus in Mark 3:5. Jesus was angry and deliberately and intentionally platted a whip to drive merchandisers out of the temple precincts. He is always angry (as is the Father) with injustice and evil. Jesus and His Father have a standing, unrelenting opposition to evil which is what *orge* means.

In this sense, the Christian is to be angry and sin not. Whenever a Christian sees little children being killed before they are born, when children and the elderly are abused, when injustice of any kind is being practiced, it is wrong to stand idly by and make no response. By the way, the leading cause of death in America is not heart disease, as we are commonly told. By a vast margin, the number one cause of death in America is the murder of the unborn.

In its negative sense, *orge* is completely condemned and forbidden because it gives birth to murder, both indirectly and directly. Selfish anger is condemned (James 1:20). Instead of resorting to physical murder, the *orge* one resorts to insulting, mocking, condemning words intending to destroy the person believed to have wronged the murderer. Such an attitude and words indicate a murderous condition of the heart. Jesus goes on to confront such speech.

The word *raca* speaks to an attitude, a tone of voice. It means to despise another in arrogant contempt. The sin of unrelenting anger is terrible; the sin of contempt is worse. Snobbery is an ugly thing whether it relates to class, intellect, financial status... it is an ugly thing of arrogance and supposed superiority. How much to be pitied is the snob.

It seems Jesus is speaking, not so much of gradations of punishments which are to be taken literally but more to illustrate how the condition of heart leads to increasingly evil and destructive behavior. Murder is ever wrong, but it is not only the deliberate taking of the life of another that is condemned but malicious slander also which is intended to destroy the reputation of another, is condemned as well. To murder, the name of another is murder in the heart.

Americans find references to common practices in church history, mainly when a "state" church existed, unbelievable. Absolute intolerance, imprisonment, torture, burning at the stake, beheading, etc., in the name of God is part of the tragic story of religious people who hold political and religious dominance. Sadly, though not as common, such practices persist in many parts of the world. More people have lost their lives because of their simple, personal faith in Jesus Christ in the past hundred years than in all of human history before.

Condemned Because Of A Conviction

An example of how those with murder in their hearts operated as Jesus taught in this text is seen in the great reformer, and those who affirmed his confession of faith. The Reformation began in 1517 when Luther, a Catholic priest, officially broke with his church and nailed his famous *95 Theses* to the door of the church in Wittenberg, Germany. He could stay silent no longer. Salvation is by grace through faith in Jesus Christ alone, not by any of the encumbrances mandated by the church. Luther's message spread like wildfire. Mind you, his sole purpose was to declare the way of salvation. He was not a revolutionary, a military zealot, a social misfit, a disturber of the peace. His only interest was to declare that peace with God was possible for anyone by faith in the finished work of Christ.

Soon, the message reached Antwerp, Belgium, Europe's most cosmopolitan capital. From Switzerland, France, England, Germany, and Europe, the message struck a chord, and thousands were soon spreading the good news. Books began to appear explaining and enhancing the message as early as 1520. Bitter opposition was instant. One Dominican friar stated he would love to fasten his teeth into Luther's throat and proudly go to the Lord's Supper with Luther's blood dripping from his lips.

Representatives of the Pope arrived in 1522 and began collecting every book on the subject that could be found for public burning. Many arrests followed. Henry Voos and Johann Eck were burned at the stake in Brussels, the first Christian martyrs of the region. The message continued to spread, and Erasmus said that though the Pope could burn the books, he could not remove the message from the hearts of believers.

Alarmed by the continuing spread of the gospel, the government issued an edict on October 14, 1529, that launched a reign of terror. Death was decreed for all heretics and any who sympathized with them. The Spanish Inquisition arrived in Flanders and continued for many years. Over 600 protestant churches were destroyed, and thousands were martyred. Today, less than one-third of one percent of Belgians are evangelical Christians.

What does Jesus want me to know?

Why does He want me to know this?

What does He want me to do in response?

Day Thirteen

"Therefore if you bring your gift to the altar, and there remember that your brother has something against you, leave your gift there before the altar and go your way. First be reconciled to your brother, and then come and offer your gift. Agree with your adversary quickly, while you are on the way with him, lest your adversary deliver you to the judge, the judge hand you over to the officer, and you are thrown into prison. Assuredly, I say to you, you will by no means get out of here till you have paid the last penny."

MATTHEW 5:23-26

So, given the dangers inherent in *orge* both in actual murder and in thoughts which are murder as well, what more should a Christian understand to live a blessed life? The practice in the Jewish community when one had done wrong—and by doing wrong, automatically disturbing one's relationship with God—was to offer a sacrifice. The Jews could easily understand what Jesus meant in these verses because it was a common practice. Acknowledging he had sinned, the person brought his sacrifice and stood at the rail where the priest would come. The sinner would place his hands on the head of the sacrifice and solemnly confess his sin and perversion, acknowledging that he had rebelled against God by specific acts of disobedience.

He then asked God's forgiveness in response to his repentance and pleaded that the sacrifice be his covering.

This—the Jew believed—restored his relationship with God.

This practice could be done as a physical activity without remorse or repentance for the sin. It could be a ritual where one said the right things with all the right words but was utterly devoid of "heart." The result was:

1. There was never an atonement for the Jews called the "sin of the high hand." It resulted in the sin being "passed over" if the sin were not deliberate and premeditated.

2. Satisfaction (passing over the sin) was possible if every effort was made to rectify the sin, including restoration. The Jews understood a response to sin carried personal responsibilities.

Jesus took the practice to another level of understanding and application. It is impossible to be right with God unless one is right with others. Sin must be confessed from the heart both to God and man. This confession is accompanied by every effort to do everything possible to repair the breach. Whether the other person responded or not, a genuine effort must be made to reconcile the breach. This is not a ritual. It is a godly motivation of love from the heart.

To this, Jesus adds some very practical instruction. The Jews easily understood his instruction since it was a common practice among them. His point was to deal with breaches quickly, thoroughly, intentionally before they led to, more significant trouble. This is instruction Jesus gives a man when he has made a summary arrest. We would call it a citizen's arrest. Among the Jews, such an arrest required specific conditions:

1. The one arrested, the *apagoge*, had been caught red-handed. The arresting one caught him by the cloak at the throat so if the offender struggled, he would strangle himself. These two are then on their way to see the judge. Offenses resulting in a summary arrest might include stealing another's clothes at the public bath, pickpocketing, kidnapping (choice slaves were a common target), etc.

2. As they go before the judge (if the offender is found guilty), he is handed over to the court officer, the *huperetes* who was to see that the offender made full restitution.

Jesus said to settle out of court. Not doing so most likely will make matters worse and worse. Some disputes last for generations. The Hatfield's and McCoy's legend comes to mind. Jesus was teaching, "Have the grace and maturity to confess your sin and do exactly what is required to make things right." Immediate action taken with a genuine attitude will almost always settle a grievance.

Jesus also taught that if one refused to respond appropriately, the matter didn't end there. It might end there at the human level, but there is still the judgment seat of God to consider. God is just. Nobody gets away with anything. In time or eternity, wrong will be dealt with. "Right" will be dealt with as well. Nothing escapes God's notice, and He rewards even a cup of water given in His name. If one would know a blessed life, he will deal with the things which involve anger quickly, decisively, and finally. Then, move on.

The new standard for kingdom living took a common human experience and revolutionized it. Offenses occur. The natural response is to angrily react. Both flaring anger and long-smoldering plans for revenge are natural. Jesus introduced a revolutionary response to anger and anger's "children" (bitterness, jealousy, hatred, etc.) Jesus' response: love. Love God and love men and express the new standard by dealing with offenses quickly, thoroughly, finally. Restore the relationship and move on.

A Message for a Murderer

In March of 1945, Corrie Ten Boom was released from Ravensbruk Concentration camp. Hardly a day passed in the camp that Corrie had not reviewed the stranger's visit who betrayed her family back at the watch repair shop. It was a bitter memory. Now released, Corrie forced herself to review the betrayal, her Christian faith, and the information she had received. She learned who the betrayer was.

She wrote a letter to the offender stating she had heard he was most likely the man who had betrayed the family. She told him of both her father and sister's death in the concentration camp and of her own ten months spent there. Then, she triumphantly declared that what her betrayer had intended for evil, God had used for good. Part of that "good" was that she could pray for a man who had brought such pain. Furthermore, she assured him that if he repented of his sin, God would forgive him—something she had already done.

In forgiving the betrayer and pointing him to the One who could deliver him from his prison, she recognized she had freed another from prison: herself. Freed from bitterness and a smoldering hatred, she carried her message across the world: "My survival is not my miracle, but the reality of Jesus." She often described herself as "... the skin on the hands of God." Thousands turned to Christ through her testimony. She wrote five books. An entire feature film, "The

Hiding Place" was made about her life. Corrie Ten Boom died at the age of 91 in 1983.[13]

What does Jesus want me to know?

Why does He want me to know this?

What does He want me to do in response?

Day Fourteen

"You have heard that it was said to those of old, 'You shall not commit adultery." but I say to you that whoever looks at a woman to lust for her has already committed adultery with her in his heart."

MATTHEW 5:27-28

Here is the second standard for kingdom living: Thou shalt not commit adultery. (Exodus 20:14) To violate this commandment meant the death penalty (Leviticus 20:10). Adultery is the negative, abusive use of a God-created characteristic in men and women. It is not the desire for sexual satisfaction but the illicit use of sex Jesus addresses. Again, there are two sides to this coin. One side of the "sex coin" is enriching, delightful, and loving. The other side is selfish and abusive.

It is natural and acceptable to take note of the attractive and desirable. At first glance, such factors are easily and naturally obvious. It is the second glance/gaze that is the problem. A lingering, deliberate look that fantasizes about having sex with that person...that is what Jesus condemned. The reason for this is the thought is parent to the act.

Human nature being what it is, it is all too easy to find a way to turn the fantasy into an immoral act of adultery.

Jesus added a whole new dimension to sexual morality. Of course, the act of adultery is sin but Jesus said the lingering thought that contemplated and fantasized about adultery is sin. Again, the thought often gives birth to the act...just don't go there.

The question is often raised in the light of this statement by Jesus: "Is it just as bad to think a thing as to do it?" At first glance, the answer might seem to be "Yes." While in no way diminishing the concept Jesus stated, the answer to the question is "No." A lustful thought is sinful. Period. However, if the lustful thought finds a way to complete itself in the physical act of adultery, that is worse than the thought itself. The reason is obvious. If kept in the mind of the mental-adulterer, only one person is involved. Should the thought be pursued until it is acted out in adultery, there are now at least two people affected. In addition, there is the probability the sin will become public knowledge and tempt others to follow suit.

A King with a Roving Eye

The power of lustful, sexual thoughts and the destruction they bring is illustrated in the life of King Henry VIII of England. His roving eye always surveyed the women around him, especially since he had no son to succeed. His marriage to Catherine of Aragon was at an end because her child-bearing years were past, and there was no son in sight. Henry determined to divorce her, especially when his lustful eye fell on a recent addition to his court, Anne Boleyn though she was only fifteen.

Still married to Catherine, Henry pressured Anne to be his mistress. When he demanded she agree to be his wife, she fell to her knees and pleaded with him not to defile himself nor her and thus bring both the wrath of the queen and God upon them. Henry would not be denied. He informed Anne that he was divorcing Catherine, after which Anne agreed to marry him after the divorce. The divorce proceeding dragged on. Henry pressured. Finally, convinced the divorce would occur someday, Anne gave in and became Henry's mistress. Eventually, the divorce was granted, and Anne became the new queen.

Henry's affection for Anne faded when after three years, she had born him only a daughter, the future Queen Elizabeth I. Henry remained true to his character and began plotting to have Anne convicted of adultery since he had decided on a new conquest, Jane Seymour. On May 19, 1536, Anne was convicted of adultery and was beheaded.[14]

What does Jesus want me to know?

Why does He want me to know this?

What does He want me to do in response?

Day Fifteen

"If your right eye causes you to sin, pluck it out and cast it from you for it is more profitable for you that one of your members perish than for your whole body to be cast into hell. And if your right hand causes you to sin, cut it off and cast it from you for it is more profitable for you that one of your members perish than for your whole body to be cast into hell."

MATTHEW 5:29-30

Different people find that different things tempt them to sin. A problem for one might be no problem to another at all. But the truth is everyone has temptations to sin. Even Jesus had such temptations. So, what guidance does Jesus give kingdom citizens regarding temptation?

The word for "offend" in this text is *skandalon*. It is a word that refers to the bait on a fishhook or the trigger on a trap. Whatever "bait" is offered, if taken, the result is the same: destruction. Jesus is concerned that we can recognize when we are being baited to sin.

Faced with a critical decision, the "bait" may take one of two forms: (1) sometimes called the sin of "omission," it is failing to do what is biblical or (2) doing what is not biblical, sometimes called the sin of "commission." In the first instance, the Christian fails to stand firm due to the fear of suffering or even death. In the second instance, the temptation is to do the forbidden: lie, deny the faith, etc. Perhaps it is a distinction without a difference, but yielding to temptation and taking the bait is always destructive, whether in the negative or the positive.

Two-word pictures are suggested in these verses. There is the picture of a stone in the path over which one stumbles or trips. The other picture is of a cunningly concealed pit. *Skandalon* is the thing that trips or traps a person destructively. Jesus is not speaking of literal action when He speaks of plucking out an eye or cutting off a hand. He figuratively to warn a person how dangerous certain things are to the kingdom citizen. Whatever lures you into a deadly trap is to be eliminated at all costs.

We immediately associate the teaching here with what has just been taught: anger and adultery. How can one eliminate such thoughts? One effort is a determination not to think about the forbidden thing. This effort will guarantee that we will lock ourselves into thinking about the offense we have suffered or the person about whom we fantasize. Another effort is the "hermit" approach: remove yourself from normal living. Isolate, avoid. One can escape the physical contact, but this does not eliminate the thought

Accepting that fact, eliminating destructive thoughts and practices will be a lifelong battle...accept that fact. Perhaps we will never succeed in eliminating such destructive thoughts in this life. The best strategy for defeating things that tempt us is thought replacement. When any destructive thought or bait asserts itself, cultivate the practice of instantly substituting the godly opposite. This is work, disciplined work, but it will eventually result in the intended evil becoming the trigger for the very opposite of what the temptation intended to accomplish: your destruction. (Philippians 4)

Leaders Cannot Hide

James Renwick was tempted to avoid arrest and imprisonment. When he realized that if he remained in hiding, he could not be a leader, he refused to hide. The Covenanters were the persecuted Scottish Presbyterians who covenanted together to declare and preserve the reformed faith in Scotland. He took a leadership position in the Covenanters when their fearless leader, Donald Cargill, was martyred.

James VII became the King of Scotland in 1685 and issued an order that worship in private homes, chapels, and places designated for worship was acceptable. All open-field and secret worship were forbidden since State Church could not regulate these services. Many ministers, tired of the struggle, accepted the compromise. Renwick did not. He continued his ministry for three years, but the government branded him a traitor and ordered his arrest. Protected by his Christian friends, he moved actively among those scattered throughout the mountains to survive. In one year, he baptized over 600.

One winter night, he was finally tracked down and arrested. He was immediately sentenced to death. The Council, hoping to benefit from the recantation of one so influential as Renwick, offered him a week to recant. Renwick wrote to his mother during that week, assuring her he was doing well. He had found peace, realizing the time of his death had come. His response to that realization was to worship the God he would soon see. He shared the same message with his

Christian friends the night before he was to be executed, stating the only thing he regretted was that he was leaving his Christian friends.

On February 17, 1688, the morning of his death, James Renwick, saw his mother and sisters in the crowd gathered at Grassmarket in Edinburgh to witness his execution. As he walked resolutely to the gallows, he declared to the crowd that death was no threat to him at all. From the gallows, James read Psalm 103 and Revelation 19, and then he prayed:

"Lord, I die in the faith that Thou will not leave Scotland but that Thou will make the blood of Thy witnesses the seed of Thy church and return again and be glorious again in our land. And now, Lord, I am ready." The last Covenanter to be hanged in public for the faith, James Renwick was 26 years of age.[15] How convicting are so many of those who have gone before us.

What does Jesus want me to know?

Why does He want me to know this?

What does He want me to do in response?

Day Sixteen

*"Furthermore it has been said, 'Whoever divorces his wife,
let him give her a certificate of divorce.' But I say to you
that whoever divorces his wife for any reason except sexual
immorality causes her to commit adultery, and whoever
marries a woman who is divorced commits adultery."*

MATTHEW 5:31-32

The first commandment in Scripture is "Be fruitful and multiply..." (Genesis 1:28). This was spoken to a married couple in the context of a marriage bond, one husband and one wife together for life. By the time Jesus arrived on earth, this bond was in danger of disappearing, even among the Jews. The very corrosive view of marriage held by the pagan Greeks and Romans became much more common.

Historically, the Jews had a high view of marriage. Only one reason was permitted for a man not to marry and have children: that he might devote himself to the study of the law. Otherwise, a man was a disgrace. The Jews heartily agreed with God in hating the whole idea of divorce (Malachi 2:16). A Jew would surrender his life rather than violate any one of three things: idolatry, murder, or adultery.

Sadly, the theory was much stronger than the practice. The greatest threat to the sacred bond of marriage was the status of women. Essentially, they had no status. A woman was a thing, absolutely at the disposal of her father or husband. She had virtually no rights. Under no circumstance could a woman divorce her husband. On the other hand, two schools of thought applied to the men in Jewish culture. One school taught that only adultery could break the marriage vow. The other school said a man could divorce his wife for any reason he pleased. Deuteronomy 24:1 was the disputed passage.

The issue was the definition of "some indecency." In the far more popular meaning (for men) the phrase meant "whatever." The writ stated: *Let this be from me thy writ of divorce and letter of dismissal and deed of liberation that thou mayest marry whatsoever man thou wilt.* With this, in the presence of two witnesses, the marriage was over.

The woman had no recourse by law. She might be able to return to her father's house and his authority, or she might resort to prostitution to survive, which is the implication of "...causes her to commit adultery." It was this widespread practice among the Jews that Jesus confronted. The human family was nearing collapse. Moral degeneration was rapidly increasing. Jesus took an extremely high view of marriage. His teaching on the subject was squarely based on marriage as God originally designed it (Matthew 19). There are both practical and moral reasons for this position, which will never change whatever secular cultures may do. Unbiased evaluation of the one man/one woman-faithful-to-each-other-for-life position shows its vast superiority over any alternate position on marriage.

Since marriage (and by extension, the home and family) involved cultures other than the Jews, the subject bears further study. Christianity would spread worldwide. What is the Christian position on marriage which was to be taught and practiced by Christians for all time? This is a critical question, given the fact that Christianity was launched into a Greek/Roman culture and was a radical departure from the common culture.

The Greek view of marriage/home/family may be summed up in the statement of Demosthenes: There are courtesans for the sake of pleasure; concubines for daily cohabitation. Wives exist for the purpose of having legitimate children and guarding our household affairs.[16]

Adultery among the Greek men was absolutely free of any stigma whatsoever. It was expected as a part of the normal flow of life. On the other hand, the Greek wife was required to have complete moral purity.

Paul encountered such moral conditions wherever his missionary travels took him. In Corinth, the subject is addressed in detail. The Corinthian culture endorsed and amazing alliance of prostitution and religion and openly displayed it. The whole social system in the Greek-controlled world was based on relationships outside of marriage. Divorce for a Greek man was official when he said it was done in the presence of two witnesses. He did not even have to return his wife's dowery.

The Roman world was dominated by the *Patria Protestas*, the father's absolute power, even the power of life and death. A Roman son was under his father's control as long as the father lived. Unlike her Greek counterpart, who lived in secluded isolation, the Roman wife took full partnership in life. Prostitutes were held in contempt. For the first five hundred years of the Roman Empire, there is not a single case of divorce recorded. The first recorded divorce was in 234 BC, and this was because the wife was childless.

By the second century BC, the descent into moral catastrophe exploded. What happened? The Romans conquered Greece militarily, but the Greeks conquered Rome morally. Divorce became as common as marriage. Women were married to divorce. Seneca stated that the name of their latest husband identified women. One woman had eight husbands in five years.

With such moral depravity regarding marriage, and the insatiable cravings of lust, particularly sexual passion, it is not surprising that the most despicable and depraved practices would come to dominate the pagan world. This found expression in rampant homosexuality (Romans 1).

To such a world, Christianity came. It was an astonishing message and practice that Christians brought regarding the sanctity of marriage. The pagan world was astonished that husbands and wives were bound by love, devotion, and fidelity...for life! Couples shared a full partnership that defined their duties, responsibilities, and roles, which they readily embraced and faithfully followed. Christian couples embraced the teachings of Jesus completely and found great security and satisfaction in them.

As stated earlier, the Jews had a very high view of marriage. Still, they were vexed by the subject of divorce. We have already mentioned the two schools of Jewish teaching on the subject–divorce for adultery only, or divorce for whatever reason the husband might choose. The Pharisees were particularly concerned about the subject and tried to trap Jesus on more than one occasion. The challenge was to interpret the Deuteronomy 24:1 passage. The Hillel school ("whatever") prevailed over the Shammai school (infidelity only).

There are many details about this discussion that I will not address. Suffice it to say those who heard Jesus teach on the subject were well versed in Rabbinic law. The common view was that divorce was mandatory when either of the two conditions existed. (1) Sterility. The purpose of marriage was offspring (Jews cited Genesis 1:28). After ten years of marriage, divorce was compulsory if a couple had no children. In such cases, a woman could remarry with all other regulations on marriage intact for the second marriage or (2) Adultery.

Two other Jewish regulations applied to divorce. (1) Desertion was never a basis for divorce. If desertion was alleged, death must be proved. (2) Insanity. Insanity was not a cause for divorce. A man who went insane could not write a writ of divorce. A woman who went insane would have no protection, so a husband could not divorce her. It was complicated. Throughout His ministry, the Pharisees attempted to trap Jesus in some contradiction or violation of the law. This is another example of their efforts. His response was astonishing and radical. To the complicated regulations that the Jews wrestled with, Jesus took them back to their law and God's original design in Genesis.

Adam and Eve were created for each other and no other. The fact that there were only the two on earth notwithstanding, the pattern is complete and unending. The union of one man and one woman, complete and unbreakable, is the pattern for all time. Each new couple is a reproduction of Adam and Eve, and the principle (not law) Jesus laid down was that divorce is a violation of that principle.

Moses provided for a bill of divorcement. Jesus said Moses was not initiating a law but a concession. Moses did not command divorce but only a concession to fallen human nature. The principle was to regulate the deplorable practices of divorce. Divorce is never commanded. The marriage union is always intended to be *kiddushin*, the Jewish term for consecration or sanctification...dedication to God as exclusive, totally surrendered. The husband/wife vow means that each has sole possession of the other. This does not just apply to sex (though that is a significant issue) but to all the things the couple shares.

According to God's design, a man and a woman are to find a merging of personalities in marriage. One is not to be so dominant that the other has no practical or shared role. Marriage is not to be a life-long power struggle as to which one is to be in control. Marriage is not meant to be a sharing of the same residence from which each goes their way, doing their own thing, being in a relationship in name only. No, marriage is a relationship that merges the vital but different identities, roles, and abilities into one harmonious life together. Marriage does not restrain life; it completes and enlarges it.

Marriage does not eliminate the personality of either partner; it enhances it. Marriage partners share all of this in the circumstances of life...the joys and the sorrows, together. The sorrows are cut in half when shared; the joys are doubled. Marriage partners see each other at their worst and their best, exclusively. Two people stand "...naked and unashamed..." in all ways and agree to go on together.

Marriage should come only after both have had the opportunity to know the other to a substantial degree. Both need to have a solid understanding of what they are getting into. Each should be reasonably clear on what life will be like when married to this person. Marriage is no light thing. Consummating the bond in the sexual union after marriage is only the crowning act the couple has found in getting well acquainted (in all ways except sexual intercourse) before the wedding day.

Reality vs. Appearances

For all the good he did in the kingdom of God, John Wesley was not wise in marriage. He thought he had found the perfect wife in the widow Molly Vazeille. He was smitten by her uncommon neatness and cleanness. She was past childbearing age so there would be no fatherhood responsibilities for John. Furthermore, she was independently wealthy, freeing him from the need to support her, while allowing him to continue to give most of his money to the poor. She was not a member of high society so there would be no prying eyes to spy on the couple as had been the case in one of Wesley's earlier love interests. Surely this was the will of God so, in January 1751, John determined he would marry Molly.

Wesley planned a preaching tour in Northern England before he decided to marry Molly. On February 10, 1751, he set out on his tour but slipped on London Bridge, spraining his ankle. Instead of a preaching tour, he made his way to Molly's home so she could care for him. During the week of his recovery, he determined he would marry her immediately. Previously, John had agreed with his brother Charles that neither of them would marry without the approval of the other. Now, John merely wrote Charles a letter announcing his decision. Charles was astonished and later commented that the event "...made us all hide our faces."

Two weeks after the wedding, John set off on his preaching tour. Molly stayed home, much to John's disappointment. Furthermore, Molly did not write for four whole days. Still, John wrote, "My body (ankle) is stronger and stronger—and so is my love for you...O, that we may continue to love one another as Christ has loved us."

Eventually, Molly did travel some with John, working among the poor to assist in the ministry, but the difficulties wore on her very quickly. Her travels and work with John faded. He did not attempt to alter his travels and ministry and expressed his expectation that Molly would show genuine compassion and godly obedience. Molly grew increasingly resentful of John's absence and developed a violent temper.

Her resentment grew, and she sought to make John's life miserable as well. She destroyed some of his writings, publicly criticized him— at times riding into the middle of a crowd gathered in an open-air service on her horse and standing as tall as possible in the stirrups, berating him while he was trying to preach. She repeatedly accused him of adultery. In 1771, Molly abruptly left. She was gone three years but finally decided to return home.

Shortly after her return, a friend of the family entered a room unannounced to find Molly dragging John (a small man) across the floor by the hair of his head. The marriage continued to deteriorate. Efforts were made to reconcile, but John was resolute in his rejection of his wife in the end. He bitterly complained that she had been a huge stumbling block to his ministry and that he was bidding her a final farewell. They never met nor spoke again. Wesley was not even informed when Molly died. He wrote in his diary, "I came to London and was informed that my wife had died on Monday in a diary entry. This evening she was buried, though I was not informed of it."[17]

If champions of the faith such as John Wesley—who lived in a day when there was a far greater commitment to the integrity of marriage—could be so unwise in matters regarding marriage, is it any wonder that immorality and divorce are so common today?

When even tractor tires are advertised by sexy models—when a particular soft drink will get the girl—when every encounter is aimed at getting the other into bed—when by sexual innuendo everything is focused on sex—who cares about the other *person*...it's what I want that matters. Who and what the other person is, the things that make a person who they are—and who they are going to be—is involved. When the only thing that matters is to satisfy my lust, how could it be expected that a marriage would last?

God's design for marriage is the unwavering standard, which Jesus made the standard for all people—Christian or not—for all time. Why? Because the foundation for human survival depends on it. The home is the foundation, and home is established when one man and one woman pledge themselves together for life. Greece and Rome fell. Internally rotten to the core. The insatiable lust for me/my pleasure (which is never enough) destroyed Greece and Rome. America is well down the road to the same destruction...rotting from within.

John the Baptist lost his head (literally) because he confronted a pagan king and his wife on their violation of God's standard for marriage. Yes, even stable pagan homes contribute to the well-being of a civilization. Yes, even non-Christians are bound by God's standard for marriage: one man, one woman, for life. Society depends on it.

What does Jesus want me to know?

Why does He want me to know this?

What does He want me to do in response?

Day Seventeen

"Again you have heard that it was said to those of old, 'You shall not swear falsely, but shall perform your oaths to the Lord.' But I say to you, do not swear at all, neither by heaven, for it is God's throne, nor by the earth, for it is His footstool, nor by Jerusalem, for it is the city of the great King. Nor shall you swear by your head, because you cannot make one hair white or black. But let your 'Yes' be 'Yes' and your 'No,' 'No' For whatever is more than these is from the evil one."

MATTHEW 5:33-37

Much about the Sermon on the Mount was the subject matter the Jews already knew. As we have seen, Jesus did two things: (1) He reviewed what they knew and commonly practiced, and (2) then He gave the information a completely new and radical application.

He now takes up the Jewish understanding and practice concerning oaths or vows. Jewish teachers taught that the world rested on three things: justice, truth, and peace. Oaths involved all three and were rooted in Exodus 20:7 "...you shall not take the name of the Lord your God in vain." An oath had nothing to do with swearing or cussing as we think of it. It meant invoking the name of God in the claim that was being made—i.e., God affirms this. Jesus said that since God owns everything. Invoking God's name in one's oath is nonsensical.

Regarding swearing, many common practices had developed by the time Jesus was on earth. There was trivial swearing which added an oath to anything, everything. This practice made an oath meaningless. In our day, "hero" is added to common behavior. The result is the word "hero" has lost its true, significant meaning. Christians who explain the simplest things as "miraculous" cheapen the genuinely miraculous. Sacred terms should be reserved for sacred things. It is not a miracle to find a choice parking space or to meet a long-absent friend. When everything is miraculous or heroic, nothing is. The Jews had made oath-swearing meaningless.

A second common practice was oath avoidance. The person who is highly skilled in almost saying something is not to be admired. To a Jew, an oath that invoked the name of God was utterly binding. An oath that did not actually use "God" in its expression was not binding. The Jews were masters at refining the practice of almost invoking God's name. In these oaths, they left a slight crack through which they could avoid being bound to their oath. It was deceptive, hypocritical, and wrong, and Jesus condemned it.

There cannot be one standard for church and another for the marketplace. The Christian life is consistent, uniform, and applicable everywhere. God is already there, whatever the occasion and is fully aware of what is happening. Christians should keep this in mind and live in a way that honors His name every day in everything. Christians don't need oaths; they serve no purpose. There was a time when a man's word was his bond. If he said it, it was as good as done; a handshake sealed the deal. In a small town in West Texas, the General Store was never locked. After hours or if the owner was absent, the community came, took what they needed, and left the payment on the counter or a note saying when they would come and pay. This applied to all, not just Christians. The owner said he never knew of losing a dime to theft. It's not complicated.

Does Jesus say in these verses that a person is not to take an oath in a court of law? Of course not. That is not His point. Some see oath-taking as a violation of Scripture. It is not. It is simply a testimony of the fallen state of man that one is required to take an oath to "tell the truth, the whole truth, and nothing but the truth" when preparing to give testimony. A simple "Yes" or "No" would be all the oath needed if things were as God intended. No evasion, partial truth, or hypocrisy, just the plain truth. Most of all—if an oath is ever required—the validity of the oath is established, not by word only, but by the life lived by the one making the oath. Maeyken Wens illustrates my point.

Cruelty Upon Crueltry

Maeyken (Mae) was the wife of an Anabaptist minister. (Anabaptists believed in believer's baptism and were forerunners of present-day Baptists). In April 1573, Mae and four others were in a Bible study in a home in Antwerp, Belgium. They were suddenly surrounded and arrested, and placed in prison under horrible conditions. Their interrogation began. When intimidation did not shake their faith in the least, the torture began.

The cycle of intimidation, deprivation, and torture continued for months to force the women to renounce their Christian convictions. Finally, having completely failed in their efforts, the council condemned them to be burned at the stake. On October 5, 1573, Mae wrote a final letter to her fifteen-year-old son, Adriane, urging him to care for his ailing father and his three-year-old brother. She urged him to remain strong in the Lord and to live to join her in heaven one day. She had a great concern for her children and repeatedly encouraged them to find their strength in the Savior. Her final words were praises for the grace God provided her as death loomed.

On October 6, Mae and the other women were prepared for execution. The executioner came to their cell and had each stick out their tongue. He placed an iron clamp over their tongue and tightened it with a vice screw. Then he burned the end of their tongue, causing swelling, which would prevent removing the clamp or saying anything at their execution. Then, they were marched to the marketplace in Antwerp.

Adrien could not stay away from his mother's martyrdom. Carrying his three-year-old brother he stared as his mother was led to the stake and tied while the firewood was stacked around her. He could stand it no longer. He fainted and did not regain consciousness until his mother and the others had been burned to ashes. He lingered after everyone else left the marketplace and searched among the ashes. There, he found his mother's tongue screw. [18]

Of Mae and millions of others like her, the words from the Book of Hebrews echo the words "...of whom the world was not worthy..." (Hebrews 11:38).

What does Jesus want me to know?

Why does He want me to know this?

What does He want me to do in response?

Day Eighteen

"You have heard that it was said, 'An eye for an eye and a tooth for a tooth' But I tell you not to resist an evil person. But whoever slaps you on your right cheek, turn the other to him also. If anyone wants to sue you and take away your tunic, let him have your cloak also. And whoever compels you to go one mile, go with him two. Give to him who asks you, and from him who wants to borrow from you do not turn away."

MATTHEW 5:38-42

Once again, Jesus took up an issue that was commonly understood. This time, the subject is the *lex talionis,* an eye for an eye, and a tooth for a tooth. It has its origin in the first known codified law, the Code of Hammurabi, which dates from 2285-2244 B.C.

This law became deeply embedded in the Jewish ethic of the Old Testament. Summarized, the principle practiced was a regulation for injury or other violation. Each violation was matched exactly by a response. The law was stated in Exodus 21:23-25 and other places. It has been practiced in all generations and is still practiced in some primitive cultures. This was the practice:

If a person from one tribe injures a member of another tribe, the entire tribe of the injured one takes vengeance on the whole tribe of the offender. Blind the eye of one in our tribe will blind the offender in your tribe. Often, revenge got out of hand, and much more injury than the original eye for an eye resulted. Actually, lex *talionis* was the beginning of mercy. Its original intent was vengeance. *Lex talionis* made the response just instead of out-of-control violence. The law deliberately limited retaliation in these ways:

1. Only the person inflicting the injury was punished, not his entire tribe. His punishment was to be the equivalent of the injury he caused or the damage he had done.

2. An individual could never act alone. His case must be brought before a judge in a court of law, Deuteronomy 19:18. The judge decided on the appropriate response to the loss or injury.

3. The law was not carried out literally because to do so could be unjust as well. For example, the injured eye might have been diseased or damaged already. To take a perfectly good eye from the violator in exchange for the bad eye of the victim would be unjust. Money or property became the exchange. Several things were taken into consideration to make a just response to the loss. Five common cases for compensation were specified: for injury, pain, healing, loss of time, and indignity.

Our laws today largely reflect these same things. There is an assessment for income loss or even loss of earning power resulting from the injury. Additional assessments are often made for pain and suffering or slander.

Though an eye for an eye is outlined in the Old Testament, there are many provisions for mercy as well (See Leviticus 19:18; Proverbs 24:29; 25:21; Lamentations 3:30). With all of these factors in view, Jesus addressed the issue of injury, loss, and responses by His followers. In His response to this common law, Jesus obliterated the acceptability of retaliation.

The Christian lives by the concepts of the beatitudes—whatever the circumstances, God is there. When skies are blue, health is good, and there's money in the bank...of course, I believe this. I can deliver pep talks with the best of them to others when their troubles grow. However, let me be severely tested, and I'm much more vulnerable to Satan's ancient question in Eden, "Is God good?"

In truth, He is good (my whining notwithstanding). He is completely aware of everything involved in the event. He always, without exception, acts justly. His action is always complete, precisely at the right time, and will always be good for His kingdom and the Christian involved. Sooner or later, most of us get the test: what will I do when any of these three examples Jesus now gives show up? If we "get it" His literal instructions will prove to be the very best response.

1. "If one smites you on the right cheek..." Do not consider this to apply to a fist to the face. Instead, Jesus is speaking of a deeper issue. Most people are right-handed. Why did Jesus speak of the *right* cheek? Because a right-handed person would have to "back-hand" a person to strike the right cheek. The point: this is an insulting, mocking act.

2. Rabbinic law stated this was doubly insulting. Jesus says a deliberate insult is not cause for the Christian to retaliate in kind. Blessed is the man who is slighted when he deserves

to be applauded. Blessed is the person who does not resent deliberate insults just as Jesus demonstrated once and again.

3. "...if anyone takes your tunic..." The Jew had two essential garments: the tunic, the inner garment made of cotton or linen, and the cloak, the large outer garment used as a blanket at night. So, a tunic for daytime use and a cloak for night comfort. Jewish law required that if the cloak were taken from a man, it had to be returned by nightfall (Exodus 22:26-27). The cloak may not be permanently taken. Jesus teaches that a Christian must not insist on his rights. He understands he is bought and paid for. His rights were bought at the price of salvation. Instead of focusing on his rights, he focuses on his responsibilities. His rights are owned by God, whose promise (Romans 8:28) is that in the end, good will come to the one who leaves his rights with God. If a cloak was kept, don't retaliate. "...go the second mile..."

Those listening to Jesus understood this phrase at once. They lived under Roman occupation. When compelled (*aggareuein*) to do something by the occupying power, the citizen had no choice but to do it. This is what the Roman soldiers forced Simon of Cyrene to do—carry the cross of Jesus. All Roman soldiers had to do was to command it, and it was done. The soldier could compel a citizen to carry the soldier's pack one mile by law. Jesus took up this common practice and gave it a radical application. He addressed the c cotizen's common response, which was that when compelled to act by a Roman: obey but with resentment and obvious anger and do only what is required and not the slightest more.

Instead of resentment and grudging duty, Jesus said the Christian attitude was to serve with cheerfulness and willingness. The Christian is not focused on his rights and freedom to do as he pleases since he is a child of God, but to focus on the character of God who took the initiative to respond to the undeserving with mercy and grace. That Christian's character is to be displayed even to the enemy—especially the enemy.

In summary, the Christian does not resent or retaliate for an insult, will not focus on his rights but his responsibilities, and will cheerfully do what is required and more. All with grace. All of this is an expression of his witness. If you are still struggling with this concept, keep reading and meditating on the Sermon on the Mount as a whole. All the teachings weave themselves into one central message that is the standard for all time.

Martyrs Together

This spirit of "...not resisting an evil person... [by human retaliation]" is illustrated by two women named Margaret. Margaret MacLachlan (a 70-year-old widow) and Margaret Wilson (an 18-year-old serving maid) were tried for their faith on April 13, 1685. They were charged with refusing to affirm that the church of God is a department of State. They had the added charges of attending field meetings and worshiping in places other than church. Prison had been a brutal time of suffering for both with little food or light and no bed.

They were ordered to receive their sentences on their knees. They refused but then were forced and sentenced to death by drowning. On May 11, they were led to the Scottish coast at low tide. They were led to posts and tied; the older Margaret, highly respected for her faith and godly lifestyle was staked further out. They were offered many opportunities to recant. The tide was coming in. Both stood firm and resolute. The older Margaret continued to pray silently with closed eyes. As the tide overwhelmed her, she went limp.

Turning to Margaret Wilson, the soldiers mockingly asked her what she thought of Christ now. As the tide rose, she began to sing Psalm 25, and then she read Romans 8:37-39 from the Bible she clung to. As the waves rose over her head, a soldier lifted her head above the waters and demanded once again that she pray for the king. And she did pray—that God would give him repentance, forgiveness, and salvation if it were His will. The angry soldier thrust her under the water, and the two Margarets met in paradise.

What does Jesus want me to know?

Why does He want me to know this?

What does He want me to do in response?

Day Nineteen

"You have heard that it was said, 'You shall love your neighbor and hate your enemy.' But I say to you, love your enemies, bless those who curse you, do good to those who hate you and pray for those who spitefully use you and persecute you, that you may be the sons of your Father in heaven; for He makes His sun rise on the evil and the good. And sends rain on the just and the unjust.

For if you love those who love you, what reward have you? Do not even the tax collectors do the same? And if you greet your brethren only, what do you do more than others? Do not even the tax collectors do so? Therefore, you shall be perfect as your Father in heaven is perfect."

MATTHEW 5:43-48

In some ways, these verses encapsulate all Jesus has been teaching. The gracious, intentional giver is an expression of God's nature. He so loved that He gave. The background of what Jesus now teaches is Deuteronomy 15:7-11. Jewish Rabbis had five principles that governed giving:

1. Giving must not be refused. To refuse to give was viewed as the same as idolatry. Refusing to give to one in need indicated

a spirit of self-serving more than serving God, Who required supporting the needy.

2. Giving must not just meet the need of the moment but must consider the humiliation poverty brings. Give enough to sustain life but give more. Give so that something like the standard and comfort to which the needy one is accustomed is provided. Who knows, you may be the one who needs support someday. Meet the need and preserve the dignity.

3. Giving must not be ostentatious. It is to be done quietly, privately. Giving for the sake of prestige, publicity, or self-glorification was abhorrent. One temple practice was the giver came and gave secretly, so no one knew who was giving. The gift was given to one the giver never knew.

4. The attitude and manner of giving must help as much as the gift itself. If one were too proud to ask for a gift, the giver would take the initiative and say, "My son, perhaps you need a loan?" understanding the loan may never be paid back but becomes a gift.

5. Giving in the right way is giving to God. Such giving is noted and rewarded by God. How God responds to the generous, right-spirited giver may take many forms, but He will always respond to one whose giving reflects His character. Loving-kindness has no limits.

It is important to note God Himself never gives indiscriminately. God never gives in a way that encourages irresponsibility or laziness. Paul emphasized that the Thessalonians who would not work were not to eat (at the expense of others). Such giving only hurts.

Be sure to see the connection between these verses and those we've just looked at. There is a flow to the message of Jesus. None of His teachings are shallow, but there is a deepening of thought as He continues to teach. It is like a stream becoming a river.

In some ways, all Jesus has taught since verse one settles into this text. Some have called these verses the core, the centerpiece around which the whole message of Jesus revolves. This is Christianity in its most mature form. This is Christianity in work clothes. His first command is about love as the basis of relationships—including love for our enemies. "Enemy" means a hateful one, our adversary. It is the same word used for Satan. What does Jesus mean by "love"?

The Greek language is marvelous. Deeply expressive, it is never content to be "bare bones" in expression. It always elaborates on a word to show its full living color. Such is the case for "love," and there are four shades of meaning in the word love in Greek.

1. ***Eros*** – Eros is passionate love, the love of a man and woman which results in sexual intercourse. It was a good word initially but came to be contaminated by selfishness. It became "lust"—illicit desires, selfish. It is not used in the New Testament.

2. ***Storge*** – This is family love, the affection between parent and child, brother and sister. It is a bond that unites the family in affection and appreciation.

3. ***Phileo or Philia*** – These terms describe the love between best friends. Warm and affectionate describe the bond between two people, which is true, enduring, and healthy.

4. **Agape** – This is the word Jesus uses in this text. It is the strongest, deepest, most unselfish, unconquerable, invincible kind of love that can be known. Jesus says this is the kind of love the Christian exercises toward every other human being. It is the kind of love God has for humanity—all of humanity.

Since *agape* is the greatest kind of love, that we must understand it as completely as possible. These are the ingredients of agape love.

1. <u>The capacity to recognize another person's needs</u> – of all creation, the human being is the neediest. Humans need more protection and provision for a more extended period than any other created animal. A few minutes after birth, the calf or colt or antelope can stand and seek nourishment...and run if necessary. Not so the human. Typically, one-third of life is taken up before the human being goes on their own. We need much attention and provision to grow up. Too many never do.

Since we are so needy, somebody has to meet our needs. This begins with someone who cares enough (loves) to study the individual's unique makeup. This is usually the parents, of course. Every person is uniquely "wired." Each parent has God-created abilities (if they apply themselves) to join in the need-meeting task. A father carries two primary responsibilities related to his family: protection and provision. A mother's instinct seems to be liberated when she gives birth. Intuitively, she seems to perceive needs before anyone else does. Joined together, father and mother have all the resources they need to bring up their offspring in a way that results in their child honoring God and serving society well. It takes both, combining their God-given uniqueness into one faithful, fruitful effort.

Wise parents who follow the teaching of Jesus and the Bible do not subscribe to the adage, "Boys will be boys." Instead, they understand that boys will be men. What kind of men depends on the training the parents provide. So, together, loving parents set out to release an adult who will be equipped to reproduce the loving home from which they came.

2. <u>Where a need is recognized, the loving one has an automatic desire to meet that need.</u> The eagerness to meet the need does not mean every desire is fulfilled. Healthy love is prepared to be as tough as is necessary. That is, to refuse to provide a resource for what one might insist is a need when a discerning one (loving) recognizes it is not a need at all, but a "greed" simply misguided. It is just as loving to deny an illegitimate "need" as it is to provide a legitimate one. The eagerness to love in healthy, helpful, and productive ways is part of agape. So, one who truly loves takes the time and does the work necessary to meet legitimate needs. See the need, meet the need...that is *agape*.

3. <u>Motivation to meet the need identified</u> – The motivation is strictly for the benefit of the one loved. There is nothing self-serving in agape love. No strings are attached. No "I love you because…" or "I'll love you if..." No recognition is expected or sought for loving.

Agape acts just because it can. There is a need, I have the resources needed, and I'm eager to meet the need simply because I can. I expect nothing in return. How could this kind of love exist? It exists because it is God's love for us. We love Him (and others) because He first loved us (John 3:16), and His love abides in us as His children.

Think about all three of these ingredients in *agape*. That is precisely how God loves us and all people. We had a legitimate need we could never meet. He had the resource for our needs. He eagerly took the initiative to respond to our needs. We could offer nothing in return. He didn't add strings to His offer because we were incapable of giving Him anything in return for His gift. The only thing left for us to do is to draw upon His love and love all people as He does. This is what pleases Him most—and blesses us.

But there is that part about loving our enemies. Jesus didn't differentiate. Love the lovable, love the unlovable. It is easy to love some people; Jesus said to love (not just the easy) but the enemy. How is that possible? Is that not what we were to God when Jesus died on the cross...enemies? When we were in the very act of lifting the high hand (fist) against God...did Jesus not die for us (Romans 5:8)? So, I'm to apply the same ingredients of agape to my enemy? Let's look more closely into a literal application of what Jesus taught about agape.

Agape is not a feeling or an emotion; it is a choice. It is not only the heart; it is the intellect and the will as well. *Agape* is only possible for the Christian because Jesus in us can love as He did. It is not natural; it is chosen surrender.

In practical terms, this means that just as God loved us—warts and all—we love our enemies. We don't first try to reform them or wait until they do better. We accept them just as they are (just as Jesus did with us) and respond to their need. Period. This is personal. Do I live this way? There is no question but that Jesus commands this. Our only choice is to obey or disobey.

What is central to our loving our enemies? Jesus said to pray for them. Before we do anything else, we pray for our enemy. Ah, what a relief. I don't have to get involved; just say a little prayer and forget about it. Wrong. We PRAY...not just "say a little prayer."

For what do we pray? First and foremost, we pray that they may repent, believe Jesus and surrender to Him. This is personal and direct, not a general "shotgun" prayer: "Lord, I pray that all of the lost may be saved." No. It is a rifle shot "Lord, I pray that _____ will be saved, and I'm committed to joining Your commitment to save him by loving him as long as it takes." Included in our prayer of commitment to love him until he repents, realizing he has no choice but to trust Jesus.

How do we pray like that? A few thoughts based on the truth that the greatest tragedy that can befall a human being is to depart this life, unsaved...to go to hell. There is NOTHING off-limits in prayer if it results in an eternal soul being saved. Pray!

1. Pray that he will be increasingly dissatisfied with his life as it has been. Pray for a restless mind and spirit. Pray that the status quo will be increasingly frustrating to him. (And while you are praying for him, pray for yourself and get ready to "... answer the hope that is within you." Often, the best response when the one for whom you are praying begins to show an interest is to start with a very clear presentation of your own salvation experience. What caused you to consider salvation, what brought you to a conclusion, what did you do to be saved, what has your life been like since receiving Jesus?)

2. Pray that God will engineer such circumstances that he will begin questioning his old objections to surrendering his life to God. Don't try to argue him into salvation. Don't give him a book or a CD. Love him and pray that God will choose just the circumstances which will cause him to realize that there's got to be more than the rut he's living in.

3. Pray that whatever/whoever he had turned to before when he was under pressure would no longer be available or satisfying. Pray that he would begin to be open to the fact that what has allowed him to escape the drawing of the Holy Spirit is no longer effective.

4. Pray for God to create the opportunity for you to befriend him on a level that will begin the process of a salvation conversation. Sharpen your presentation of the gospel. Expect God to respond; be watching.

5. Pray that God will do whatever He has to do to get the attention of the lost one for whom you are praying. Think about that. What if that means he will have a life-threatening injury, illness, or event happen in his life? It's better than hell. What if he loses his family or his reputation? It is better than hell. What if ___ (you fill in the blank)? It's better than hell. Do you believe that? Then get on your knees until he's saved! That's so harsh, you say? Really?!

Once God answers your prayer and your friend surrenders to Jesus, he is your baby. You have just entered a demanding, joyful opportunity to help raise a baby Christian into a fully devoted follower of Christ! In your discipling process, you, along with the Holy Spirit, will take one who knows virtually nothing of what it means to be a Christian and begin aligning them with God's eternal purpose for their life. That is what LOVE YOUR ENEMY means.

Have you noticed that it rains on the just and the unjust...on the Christian's farm, and the community reprobate? Have you noticed that God shines His favor on our "Christian" nation and pagan societies as well? Jesus said that the Lord is good to all. Go thou and do likewise. (Luke 10:37). In so doing, we shall prove ourselves to be God-like people...we love as God does. And, in so doing, we become perfect. What? Perfect? It can't be. What do you mean, Jesus?

The word for "perfect" is *telios* which has nothing to do with abstract, philosophical perfection. To be perfect is to be full grown. A sacrifice worthy of being offered to God is examined and found to be without blemish...perfect. The mature, wise man is not a child. He has reached adulthood—the intended goal. To be perfect is to reach the state God intends us to reach–an adult in wisdom and behavior. It is to reach the level for which the person was designed. While not completely perfect yet, the intent of the disciple is to be actively engaged and well advanced in reaching the goal of completed maturity. They are committed to achieving the goal to be all who God saved them to be.

This is precisely what God had in mind from the beginning (Genesis 1:26). We are intended to be exactly who God created us to be—like Him. That is why we *agape* God, others, and our enemies. The most God-like thing in us is that we love the way He loves. He loved us when we were the most unlovable and when we least expected it.

Even though we know better, sometimes we struggle to see Bible characters as "real." Yes, we know they are real people with very human qualities; still, they are listed in the Bible. It seems like such people are not like us ordinary Christians. That's why I have researched to find legitimate examples to illustrate whatever truth Jesus is teaching. Examples of people just like us. To illustrate the extraordinary teaching of Jesus we have just considered, I thought of this Native American.

Love Your Enemy?

Most of us have heard the name "Squanto" and connect it to the beginning of Thanksgiving celebrations in America. Squanto was indeed involved with the settlement of early America. You may not know the rest of his story, which illustrates Jesus' teaching on loving/ serving your enemy.

Squanto was captured by Captain George Weymouth and taken to England as a slave in 1605. After spending nine years in England and learning the English language, he returned to his people (the Patuxent of Cape Cod) in 1614 on board a vessel captained by John Smith. Hardly had he become reacquainted with his people when a member of Captain Smith's expedition, Captain Thomas Hunt, lured Squanto and twenty-six other unsuspecting Indians on board his ship under the pretext of trading with them. Once on board, the Indians were clamped into irons. Captain Hunt took them to Spain and sold them as slaves. In the providence of God, Squanto met a local group who introduced him to the Christian faith. Most of the others died far from their native land.

Squanto did not remain in Spain long. He managed to make his way to England, where he found passage on a ship with Captain Dermer and sailed for America once again. When he arrived back in New England in 1619, he discovered that smallpox had ravaged his tribe in 1617. Not one member of his tribe survived.

In November 1620, Pilgrims arrived at Cape Cod and settled in a place they named Plymouth, the name of the town from which they departed in England. The Pilgrims had refused to conform to the Church of England and, under persecution, fled to Holland where they could worship freely. Still longing to build a new life, they departed from Holland twelve years later, making the voyage to the new world searching for permanent religious freedom.

After a devastating winter, much sickness, and many deaths, the Pilgrims were a discouraged lot. One day in March, an Indian appeared in the Pilgrim encampment. His name was Samoset, and he had learned some English from fishermen he had met along the Maine coast. From him, the Pilgrims learned that the land where they had settled had been the homeland of a large, savage tribe of Indians known as the Patuxent who had viciously attacked the white men who came to their land. Now smallpox had destroyed them.

After the smallpox pandemic destroyed the Patuxent, no other Indian tribe would occupy the homeland from fear the death curse might well come upon them. So it was that the Pilgrims arrived at the one habitable place on the East Coast that was safe from attack, had already been cleared and prepared for essential cultivation, and from which they might have the freedom to worship God as they wished. It was the very land where Squanto had grown up. *(Did not Jesus teach not to retaliate or resent those who mistreat you? Did not Jesus teach that if one obeyed His teaching, He would take care of the faithful one? Is Romans 8:28 not true?)*

On March 22, 1621, Samoset introduced the Pilgrims to his friend. The friend's name was Squanto. Squanto brought news that the great Indian Chief Massasoit, chief of the Wampanoag (and most of the other tribes of the area), was coming later that very day to meet the Pilgrims. With Squanto serving as the mediator/translator, the Pilgrims and the Wampanoag entered a peace treaty that lasted for decades.

As mentioned earlier, the winter of 1620-21 was a devastating time for the Pilgrims. Nearly half had died because they had no survival skills in the new world. They were in desperate straits. Squanto settled among them and taught them how to successfully plant corn, catch fish in the streams and identify and harvest the food supply of their new world. "... (Squanto) was a special instrument sent from God for our good... [then in typical British under-statement, one Pilgrim recorded in his diary] ...beyond our expectations."[19]

You don't need me to point out how easy it would have been for Squanto to say, "After what they have done to my people and me, let them die. Help work out a lasting peace!? Let them get what's coming to them!" Never would he have guessed that his expression of the Christian faith would survive and inspire for all of time.

What an astounding body of instruction we have in this one chapter of the Bible! Over and over again, we hear Jesus say, "You have heard it said, but **I** say to you." How desperately we need to listen to what Jesus has to say. Books and what men say have value...usually. But how we need to stand on the Mount of Transfiguration at humble, reverent attention as the Father says, "This is my beloved Son— hear Him!"

Meditate in His Word repeatedly by dawn's early light. Let the Holy Spirit surface the "orders of the day" and go out to the marketplace and BE that. You will find a blessed life as you do.

What does Jesus want me to know?

Why does He want me to know this?

What does He want me to do in response?

Day Twenty

"Take heed that you do not do your charitable deeds before men, to be seen by them. Otherwise, you have no reward from your Father in heaven."

MATTHEW 6:1

Having presented the magnificent message which detailed the attitude (or spirit) the Christian is to manifest throughout their life, Jesus now addresses a universal question held by men: "What's in it for me?" If I could live the beatitudes consistently in the marketplace, what would my reward be? Why live such a challenging life?

That is a natural, universal question, isn't it? Two fundamental points apply: what a person does and why they do what they do. Act and motive: Jesus addresses both. He addresses the three most significant acts of the Jewish religious life: charitable giving, prayer, and fasting. All three were well known to Jesus' audience. Anticipating the question, "Why should I live the life you describe, Jesus?" He answers.

First, Jesus acknowledges the principle of reward in Christian living. In Matthew 6:4, 6, and 18, He clarifies that reward is a factor God recognizes and approves. Goodness for goodness' sake is praiseworthy...virtue is its reward. True enough, but that is not what

Jesus is about to teach. Instead, He builds on Matthew 10:42 and 25:14-30, which is the theme of what He now presents: rewards and punishment are built into life on earth. Why is that?

First, goodness which achieves no end is meaningless. Unless a thing is good for something, it is good for nothing. Second, without reward and punishment, the good man and the bad man are the same. There is no reason for a man to live one kind of life rather than another. In modern times, the destructive application of "...no grades will be given...no score will be kept... everybody gets the same trophy... there are no winners or losers (there are only participants)" is evident. Forget it. It is meaningless to simply participate.

We conclude that both the Father and the Son were very much concerned with rewards and punishment; therefore, we must understand what Jesus means when He speaks of reward. Jesus never considered rewards to be confined to material things. The prevailing Jewish view was the Old Testament view. Rewards proved a man was good. His fields were fruitful, his flocks and herds increased, his children were numerous, and his fortune was great. That is exactly the contention in the book of Job. Jesus acknowledged the idea that goodness and prosperity were linked, but there are much more than just material things to be considered. As always, Jesus taught the deeper, more fundamental meaning.

The second consideration of reward for goodness, "good" as God defines it, is that a reward never comes to those who are preoccupied with it. The natural basis for reward is the law. If one does ___, it is written and natural law that the reward is ___. I have done so much; what is my reward? Peter once voiced this directly, "Lord, we have given up everything. What will our reward be?" (Matthew 19:27).

Jesus took the issue deeper: not law, but love. (A review of *agape* love applies here.)

The great paradox of a Christian's reward is that those who calculate what is due them for their goodness receive only a shallow reward. The person whose only motive is *agape* love never considers what they will get out of it. That person gets the greater reward. Reward, then, is at the same time the product and final goal of the Christian life.

Well then, what do these greater rewards for the Christian look like? The first aspect of valid reward is the peace and satisfaction the Christian gains from being and doing good. There is a level of contentment and joy which comes to the spiritually-minded person that can be experienced no other way. No earthly currency comes close to the payoff of *agape*-based goodness.

A doctor gaining a fortune from their practice gives it all up to go to a third-world country to serve. A nurse gives up the comfort and security of America to live in the slums, receiving children abandoned to a life of misery and pain. She seeks only the well-being of these begging, innocent children. A businessman leaves his construction company with all of its benefits to go to a disaster zone to build basic shelters for those who have nothing. A war veteran organizes fellow veterans to use their military training and experience to be first responders after a hurricane. Why? What's up with that kind of behavior? Simply, it is the Christian thing to do. Rewarded? Yes! A thousand times over but not for anything material or the headlines.

Beyond the simple joy, which is the reward for doing the Christian thing, there is a paradox: the more one does, the more that is heaped upon them. There is never a time when it gets easier. "Come to me you who are weary and heavy laden, and I will give you rest...take my yoke..." (Matthew 11:28). Really!? I know what a yoke is. How does that link with the rest? Which is it, rest or a yoke? Jesus said it is both. Isn't there something inherently recognizable in this principle? What does the coach do when he discovers an exceptional athlete? Does he make it easier for the athlete? No, the coach makes the training harder. The same is true for gifted students. When Jesus finds the right attitude in a Christian, He adds to their challenge. To whom much is given, much is required. Simply put, the reward in life is more work to do.

Finally, the greater reward is that the faithful Christian fellowships more and more intimately with God. Better and better, we know Him until, at last, we pass into His nearer presence. Blessed are the pure in heart, for they get to see God.

What does Jesus want me to know?

Why does He want me to know this?

What does He want me to do in response?

Day Twenty-One

"Take heed that you do not your charitable deeds before men, to be seen by them. Otherwise, you have no reward from your Father in heaven. Therefore, when you do a charitable deed, do not sound the trumpet before you as the hypocrites do in the synagogues and the streets, that they may have glory from men. Assuredly I say to you, they have their reward. But when you do a charitable deed, do not let your left hand know what your right hand is doing, that your charitable deed may be in secret, and your Father who sees in secret will Himself reward you openly."

MATTHEW 6:1-4

Now, let's take up the first of the three great pillars upon which the good life rests: charitable giving. In particular, Jesus addressed the motive underlying such giving. The natural and most seen charitable giving was focused on being praised and lauded for generous giving. For example, the common practice was to change a hundred-dollar bill into one-dollar bills, go to the street corner where four-way traffic was greatest and begin flinging dollar bills into the air.

The people understood the teaching of Jesus because that was exactly what the Pharisees did. The people would scramble for the money while looking admiringly at so great a man who generously gave of his wealth. Jesus said that man gets all the reward he will ever get right then and there. The flattery of men was his only reward. God has no part in it.

Giving to be recognized, flattered, and praised has its reward, but it is mighty shallow and fleeting. The Greek word *apechein* is a commercial term that means "paid in full." Your ostentatious giving will receive full and final payment in the fleeting flattery of men. How sad that one would settle for so temporary a reward and miss the eternal reward of giving to glorify God alone.

Almsgiving was the most sacred of Jewish religious practices. The Jews used the same word, *tzekekah,* for almsgiving and righteousness. Giving alms was considered a greater thing than offering a sacrifice.

The rabbis, just as Jesus, taught that almsgiving was to be done in secret. The rabbis considered the one who gave alms in secret to be greater than Moses, and Moses was their greatest prophet. There was a room in the temple called the Chamber of the Silent where people went and secretly left money. Poor families in need could come and take what they needed from the alms given there.

Human nature being what it is, the practice did not match the precept. Far too often, hypocritical persons who pretended their giving was out of compassion for the poor had no compassion at all. They did what they did for the self-glory. These were the ones Jesus denounced.

What motivates a person to give? Honestly, the desire to be praised probably tops the list. As much as one might deny it or even grieve over feeling such a need, it still lies at the root of what motivates almsgiving (charitable giving.) There are other motives.

Some give out of a sense of duty. Early American leaders had what was called nobless oblige, the responsibility of the nobility. One who had found significant material favor felt an obligation to contribute to the wellbeing of the community. In simplest terms, such giving is done for Girl Scout cookies or an FFA project. Businessmen and companies add premiums to a prize-winning calf or pig. The city fathers kick in for a community project. You have resources, it is your civic duty to share. As laudable as such giving is, by far the greater giving is not what one has, but oneself. This is often the thing missing in duty-based giving.

Though it is not common, true almsgiving or charitable giving comes from an "I get to" attitude. It is simply a motivation that rises out of identifying legitimate needs and using the resources one has to meet the need. No moral editorializing lectures are attached.

I know an older man who has continued to work well beyond retirement years because of what he calls the "Ephesians 4:28 principle"—"...that he may have something to give those in need." The man has what he needs and lives a simple, comfortable life. His philosophy is, "Who needs more stuff?" Instead, he prays and watches for legitimate needs and gives secretly to see the need met. This is giving done simply for the joy of giving as God does. This is what Jesus is teaching. "...Though (Jesus) was rich, yet He became poor for our sake so that by His poverty we might become rich" (II Corinthians 8:9)

What does Jesus want me to know?

Why does He want me to know this?

What does He want me to do in response?

Day Twenty-Two

"And when you pray you should not be like the hypocrites. For they love to pray standing in the synagogues and on the corners of the streets, that they may be seen by men. Assuredly, I say to you, they have their reward. But you, when you pray, go into your room, and when you have shut your door, pray to your Father who is in the secret place; and your Father who sees in secret will reward you openly. And when you pray, do not use vain repetitions as the heathen do. For they think that they will be heard from for their many words. Therefore, do not be like them. Your Father knows the things you have need of before you ask Him."

MATTHEW 6:5-8

According to the rabbis, by praying in secret at home, one was building a iron wall around his home. To the Jew, prayer was extremely important, so much so that it could not be trusted to spontaneous responses during the flow of life. It had to be formalized in what, when, and how it was to be practiced.

The first Jewish prayer requirement was the *shema based* on Deuteronomy 6:4-9, 11:13-21, and Numbers 15:37-41. The word *shema* means "to bear' and centers on the thought: "Hear O Israel, the Lord our God is one Lord." Every morning, the shema was to be said as soon as it was light enough to distinguish blue from white. It was to be repeated before 9:00 p.m. No exceptions. Most loved the *shema*. In time, many simply ritualized it or mumbled through it in much the same way many families ask for the blessing at mealtime or repeat the Lord's Prayer. Essentially, such a practice made the "prayer" meaningless.

A second prayer practice by the Jews was the *shemoneh esreh* which means "the eighteen." It consisted of eighteen prayers—a part of every synagogue worship service. The law was that the *shemoneh esreh* was repeated three times a day. Again, as lovely as the content is, the practice became ritualistic, garbled, and essentially meaningless.

Then there were structured prayers for all occasions—before/after meals, for light, fire, the moon, good news, new furniture...the list is nearly endless. The intent was to involve God in everything. With the best of intentions, the "heart" of the prayer was destroyed, and all that remained were beautiful but meaningless words.

The Jews are by no means the only ones who have lost the essence of both private and public prayer. Every aspect of the Christian worship experience may be reduced to duty, ritual, and time constraints. Prayer regulations may be set: prayer is to be to the Father, by the Holy Spirit, through the Son. Form and structure can squeeze the meaning out of prayer. Prayer tends to be reserved for specific times, places, and occasions. Early Christians continued to go to the temple to pray at certain times (Acts 3:1). To go to the temple to pray was not the problem; the problem was with the people who prayed. It still is.

The Jews believed in long prayers because they were taught that long prayers were more likely to be heard. In our time, we sometimes hear: "He prays such a beautiful prayer." This is not necessarily a compliment. Part of the reasoning for praying at length was a strange idea that God will grow weary and finally give in if we pray long enough. Another misconception about prayer is that the more people praying, the greater the probability that God will give us what we ask. A thousand prayers, prayed fervently, for the wrong reason are no more effective than a single prayer, prayed for the wrong reason. James said that we have not because we ask not or are praying for personal advantage, not for God's glory (James 4:3). Praying with—as it were—a gun held to God's head ("If you don't answer this prayer as I ask, I'm done with You.") is both an insult to God and quite dangerous.

Prayers may be said, they may be read, but prayers that God responds to are prayed; prayed from a heart of unwavering devotion and trust that God will respond in the right way at the right time. Prayed is made to God and against the devil and his demons. Pray in such a way that He is glorified and His kingdom is advanced. Pray with fervor (earnest, heart-felt, continuing). Such a prayer is accompanied by a heart committed to staying with God, whether His response to prayer is positive or not.

The Jews also practiced extensive repetition in their prayers. Certain words or phrases repeated repeatedly tend to have a hypnotizing effect. This repetition sometimes took the form of piling up as many adjectives as possible and adding them to God's name. One such prayer began "Blessed, praised, and glorified, extolled, honored, magnified and lauded be the name of the Holy One." One Jewish prayer had sixteen adjectives attached to the name of God.

These long, structured, ritualistic, repetitive prayers, common in Jewish practice, culminated in the last kind of "prayer" offered by the Jews. It is the prayer equivalent of the hypocritical to-be-seen-by-men almsgiver.

The one caught up in the quest to be seen as the most piously devoted to God calculated where he would pray. Mandatory prayer at 9:00 a.m., noon, and 3:00 p.m. offered an opportunity. Choosing the choice spot on the steps of the temple, in the city square, or on the street corner (where people would come from all four directions) The hypocrite prayed long, loud, head bowed, arms raised, hands stretched, palms upward. The wiser rabbis utterly condemned these practices. The Jews were taught that four types of men never find the face of God: mockers, hypocrites, liars, and slanderers. Rather than being heard for their ostentatious displays in prayer, those who prayed were heard only when their heart was attuned to God.

Jesus laid down two fundamental principles of prayer:

1. Prayer is offered to God, period. Jesus condemned prayer offered to men, not to God. There is only one consideration for the one praying: that his heart is in alignment with God's heart so that what is being done in heaven may be done on earth.

2. The one praying must never forget that God is more willing to respond to prayer than the one praying can imagine. His gifts and grace are not pried out of the hands of an unwilling being. Response to a God-honoring prayer is from a loving Father. Whatever the occasion of a believer's prayer, when prayer flows from a heart that only wants the will of God to be done on earth as it is being done in heaven, that person can be assured that at the right time and in the right way, God will respond. While waiting for God's response, the believer

presses on living out a godly lifestyle, thanking God for what He is doing in to answer to the prayer already prayed.

One more thing. Read what follows very carefully because your first impression may very well be, "This is utter heresy." A religious culture concerning prayer has grown over time. By that, I mean certain prayer convictions are just assumed to be true. I want to look at three of what I'm calling religiously cultural convictions.

1. There is power in prayer.

2. Additional power in prayer is added by the number of people praying about a matter.

3. The sincerity and fervency of those praying have much to do with a successful outcome.

None of these three are true. There is no power in prayer. Every human being has religious convictions, and prayer is common in all of them. At Mt. Carmel, the priests of Baal, the whole bunch, joined in prayer and demonstration as they sought a response to their offering on the alter. In Jonah's day, the sailors prayed mightily to their god for deliverance from the storm that engulfed them. There are many other examples. None of those prayers had any bearing on the outcome. Numerous ones prayed with fervor, and sincerity. Nothing happened. We should ask, "Why?"

Prayer is just words. Unless those words are directed to the Living God, fully aligned with His will, with no motive except His glory—they are just words. There is no power in prayer. <u>There IS power in God.</u> He is the only source.

Unless those who join in prayer are "on praying ground"—in a spiritual condition to be heard by God—and are aligned with His will as revealed in Scripture, a million can be "praying" and there will be no effect.

Sincerity and fervency, indicating a heart like God's, are of great value, James said in James 5:16. So, hear what I am saying about the power, community, and fervency of prayer. God <u>releases</u> Himself into the matter for which we pray when we are attuned to His will, way, and timing; all for His glory...and an absolute steadfastness to stay steady with Him if we never have a response to our prayer.

By Prayer and Faith Alone

Most devoted followers of Christ know the name George Muller. Most know him as a man of deep prayer and faith. Most don't know that he began training to be a Lutheran minister in his early days. At the same time, he was training to be a minister; he led a degenerate life of petty thievery and related activity. At age twenty, a friend invited George to a prayer meeting in a private home. He was intrigued that these simple people, in their Bible teaching, singing, and praying, possessed something beyond what he knew, though he was much better educated than they. That night, George left the meeting with God at work in his heart. Soon, he came to peace with God.

In 1829, he moved to London to train as a missionary to the Jews. While there, he became acquainted with a group known as the Plymouth Brethren. George became convinced of their teaching. Over the next few years, he ministered to several Plymouth Brethren congregations. At an earlier time, while studying in Germany, George became aware of work with orphans led by August Francke.

On November 21, 1835, after reading a book on Franke's life, he determined he would begin an orphanage in Bristol, England. Within five months, the orphanage was operational in response to George's prayer that God would provide a building, funds to operate the orphanage, and godly people to manage it. From the beginning, he determined he would trust God, and God alone, for the means for operating the orphanage. He never made a public appeal. His ministry is legendary, and a couple of examples represent the extraordinary response of God to his prayerful intercession on behalf of the orphanage.

On November 21, 1838, a check of the funds revealed not even one halfpenny available to buy bread for the evening meal. At 1:00 P.M. George called the staff together to pray on behalf of the need. Then he told the staff, "We will wait to see what the Lord will do."

Feeling some need for exercise, George had not gone twenty yards from the orphanage when a Christian brother handed him five pounds. The children had bread for the evening meal.

In another instance, exactly one year later, his diary reveals that there was enough money for breakfast the following day, but none for the evening meal. At the staff meeting that day, he used Matthew 6:34 as his devotional text, "... 'the morrow shall take thought of the things of itself. Sufficient unto the day is the evil thereof.'" He then recorded in his diary: "We separated very happy in God, though very poor, and our faith much tried."

Two and one-half hours before dinner the next day, a large box was delivered to the orphanage with several items which could be sold and the money used to feed the orphans. Once more, God had provided for the "...least of these, (His) little ones." Many other examples are recorded in the diaries of this remarkable man of faith and prayer.[20]

Jesus sums up the subject of prayer with what is commonly called the Lord's Prayer, which is more accurately known as the Model Prayer. (The Lord's Prayer is John 17). In these few phrases, Jesus summarizes with the most incredible simplicity, the totality of the God/believer connection. In this profound model for prayer, Jesus teaches us to bring our entire life to God's real life...to bring the whole of God into the whole of life on earth.

In profound simplicity, what prayer is and involves is displayed. We see the same wisdom and incredible expression of God's engagement in the world as outlined in the Ten Commandments. Only the mind of that Perfect, Infinite Being in Whom all things have their source, support, and end could these two grand eternal pronouncements come.

Prelude to the Model Prayer

Before getting into a detailed examination of the prayer, I thought it might be good to give some general observations of what the prayer life is like for the typical Christian. These reflections come from listening to people pray over fifty-plus years of ministry. It's embarrassing, but we all know we often pray without praying. We have learned to cobble together religious words and phrases that years of experience have provided. At a moment's notice, we can pray a beautiful prayer to man's ears, not God's.

Prayer is work. It requires study, discernment, careful listening, and Spirit-filled discipline which enables us to know if we can pray in faith. Everybody prays. The Muslim prays several times a day, facing

Mecca with his head on the floor. The Jews pray regularly, repetitively, and liturgically. The Catholics pray using their rosary and their Hail Marys. Yes, all of us pray but do we pray as God intends us to pray?

The first thing Jesus does in the Model Prayer is teach us how NOT to pray. Prayer is not an isolated event, aloof from life. True prayer engages God and reality in the trenches of daily living. In prayer, we reveal who we believe God is, who we think we are, and His disposition toward us.

We define who we believe God is more in prayer than in teaching or preaching. Suppose you want to know what a person thinks, listen to them pray. In prayer, we reveal our assumptions and convictions, our priorities and God's, our doctrine and theology. God's priorities primarily focus on the eternal—ours, mainly on health and wealth (the temporary.)

Typically, praying today reveals that we, consciously or not, are:

1. trying to convince God to do what He otherwise would not do

2. trying to inform Him

3. trying to regulate or make a deal

4. preaching to someone "who needs it" and hasn't responded yet.

This is not prayer.

Furthermore, prayer is NOT a means for expressing our own opinions or preferences. It is NOT a means for relief from stress, fear, or anxiety...a kind of pop psychology with religious overtones. Prayer is NOT an attempt to persuade God to give us what we want:

"My will be done, not Thy will be done." Prayer is NOT filling in the gaps of God's understanding.

No, prayer does not change God; true prayer changes us. There is no power in words we call prayer. The power is in/with God, and faithful prayer simply releases that power in response to the prayer aligned with God's character and purpose. A thousand prayers by powerful and prominent people are meaningless unless they are aligned with God as He is. Response to prayer does not come in proportion to the number of people who pray or with what fervency they pray. Response to prayer comes when God is free to flow His will and purpose out through His partners who are aligned with Him on earth.

As we shall see, Jesus chose three common areas of "prayer"—almsgiving, fasting, and prayer—to teach us what prayer is NOT and what prayer IS. Disciples (and only disciples) are to pray, and they are to do so not as the hypocrites do, in empty, voluminous phrases nor in public ostentatious display. We can pray for God's glory in privacy and humility or publicly and pridefully. We can't do both.

Having introduced how NOT to pray, Jesus turned to true prayer. An active prayer life is assumed because there is no ongoing intimacy with God without it. A prayerless life is unthinkable. God, Himself, is the reward for disciples who pray. That reward comes about as God rearranges our theology as we pray.

How does He rearrange our theology and align His disciples with Himself and His purposes? He sets the parameters and regulations of our worship. Where do we start? We start with "our" not "my" God. Yes, He is personal, but Jesus is teaching about public prayer.

Both relationship and fellowship with God and people are high priorities with God. His character and ours are His focus. You can have neither relationship nor fellowship with God and ignore people. God is "our" God; we are in this together. Note that "our" is the pronoun in the Model Prayer, not "I" or "my." He is the God of my brothers and sisters with whom I identify and worship. Prayer is not centered on you or me but on "our" God. So...

What does Jesus want me to know?

Why does He want me to know this?

What does He want me to do in response?

Day Twenty-Three

"In this manner, therefore, pray: our Father in heaven, hallowed
be your name. Your kingdom come. Your will be done on earth
as it is in heaven. Give us this day our daily bread. And forgive
us our debts, as we forgive our debtors, and do not lead us into
temptation, but deliver us from the evil one. For yours is the
kingdom and the power and the glory forever. Amen."

MATTHEW 6:9-13

In the previous section, we saw how the Jews piled adjective upon adjective when addressing God. Contrast that with how Jesus addressed His Father in prayer: "our Father..." That's it. The only adjective He ever used when approaching God in prayer was "Holy Father."

We sit at the feet of the Master Teacher. No other aspect of the Christian life is so carefully addressed by Jesus as is prayer. Somehow His disciples sensed the transcending role of prayer, so they said, "Lord, teach us to pray..." (Luke 11:1). They did not say, "Lord, teach us to preach, witness, heal, give, etc." Unless a disciple's life is aligned with God, no Christian activity matters. Only that which can flow out of heaven into action on earth through an aligned Christian matter. So, indeed Lord, teach us to pray (to do it) AND teach us how to do it. So, let's set a context.

1. Prayer can only be done by a disciple. Though the crowd heard the teaching, it was directed to the disciples. Prayer can only be effective when the one praying knows God and knows what he is doing.

2. Prayer has a design. The first three considerations in the Model Prayer are directed to God and His glory. The second three considerations have to do with the disciples' needs and necessities.

3. Prayer is never meant to bend or persuade God to our will. It is always to align our will with His. This alignment allows for God's timing and shaping His response to His kingdom plans. It acknowledges that there is more going on in kingdom work than the disciple knows. The disciple simply prays the burden of his heart (which God originates anyway, Psalm 37:4) and trusts God to respond in the right way, at the right time.

4. Prayer acknowledges that God has chosen to include the disciple in His work; disciples are necessary. God could do kingdom work without disciples but has chosen not to do so.

5. Prayer is practical. Man has three basic needs: bread, the need to give/receive forgiveness, and help with the temptation. Bread for our physical life comes from God's sustaining grace. Forgiveness was received and continues to be possible by the finished work of Christ. The power to resist and overcome

the pressures of temptation is provided by the Holy Spirit, our Guide, and Guardian.

6. Prayer is THE absolute priority of the Christian life. "The weapons of our warfare are not carnal [physical] (weapons of flesh and blood) ..." (II Corinthians 10:4-5). This means that legislation, petitions, protests, websites/blogs/social media, a new strategy against evil, etc., is not the answer to the spiritual darkness that sweeps over our world. Why? Because our war is not with flesh and blood (Ephesians 6:12a).

Satan is never more concerned and engaged in spiritual warfare than when a Christian is praying upon the basis of Jesus' teaching on the subject. There is no more significant threat to Satan's strategy than a Christian aligned with God to advance His kingdom. Satan brings his most deceptive weapons to the prayer battle, knowing the danger of genuine prayer. Distractions, doubts about the effectiveness of prayer, questions as to "is this prayer generated by God or by me", etc. are Satan's common efforts to subvert prayer.

But someone questions, "Didn't Jesus say Satan was defeated, and his judgment sealed as a result of His finished work?" (John 16:11). How can you say Satan is behind the evil in this present world; maybe it is just the nature of the world? The world is fallen, and Satan uses it gleefully.

The Bible indeed teaches that Satan's doom is already sealed; he is sentenced to the lake of fire (Matthew 25:41, Revelation 20:10). However, though Satan's end is as inevitable as if it had already happened, the end has not come yet. Meanwhile, he marches through the world, seeking whom he may devour. After all, Satan manages the events of the world. Though Adam and Eve were assigned that responsibility, they forfeited it in Eden, and Satan has managed the world ever since. Remember, Jesus did not correct Satan (Luke 4) when he claimed to be able to deliver the whole world over to Jesus if Jesus would fall and worship him.

Therefore prayer is THE priority of the Christian life. By true, real, fervent prayer, the means for defeating the enemy is revealed. Again, Satan knows this, and that is why he has deceived even sincere Christians into a mad pursuit of "spiritual" activities, conferences, studies...anything that will leave no time for fervent prayer. Failure to make prayer THE priority is the greatest failing in Christianity today.

Maybe a recent experience I had will explain this more clearly. I needed to get something from our safety deposit box at the bank. I took my key, the lady at the bank took hers, and we went to the vault. She inserted her key; I inserted mine and turned the keys together. The box opened. God has inserted His key...we just have not inserted ours. Everything is in place. The deal is done, but we are losing by default because we don't insert the prayer key (not really). Prayer is a partnership with God. He will do His part. The question is, "Will we do ours?"

What does Jesus want me to know?

Why does He want me to know this?

What does He want me to do in response?

Day Twenty-Four

"Father, in heaven..."

MATTHEW 6:9

God is that perfect, infinite being in whom all things have their source, support, and end. It is to that one unique supreme being that we pray. The heathen is tormented by confusion and fear as to gods. There are countless gods to acknowledge and appease. How can a person know if he has done the right thing, to/for the right god? Has he done enough? Has he missed a god, and has he understood what satisfies each one? It drives a person mad.

1. Jesus said there is only one God. He is the God of all people, all things, and He is the God who loves. His greatest desire is for every man to know Him as a loving Father. He wants a personal relationship with the ones He created in His image.

2. In addition to the Father's desire for a relationship with us, He wants us to know that He has designed the world so that we, His children, might be trained to partner with Him in advancing His kingdom. He has the capacity and purpose of using every circumstance in life as part of this training. In every circumstance, His goal is His glory and our good.

Prayer is the primary way to maintain this perspective when life gets painful and difficult.

3. He is the Blessed Controller of all things. He desires to partner with us in establishing and advancing His control—a control that is always in love. Then He desires that all of His disciples move from "me" to "we" ...to grow up in our love for our fellow man and our Father: OUR Father...forgive US. Lead US.

"Our Father who is in heaven..."

All that has been said about God is true. He is a loving father. But He is so much more. He is in heaven, and He is holy. He is not "...the man upstairs." He is not my buddy. He is not a religious Santa Claus or an indulgent grandfather. He is not a divine rabbit's foot. He is God. Jesus seldom used the word "Father," probably out of reverence for God. True, God is love and makes it very clear that we may approach Him as a Father, but such an approach is always with reverence and most profound respect. In praying "Our Father in heaven..." we recognize at the same time His love and power. In love, He moves, and He moves powerfully. In Him, "...ALL things have their source, support, and end." that is His power.

"Hallowed be Thy name..." (Let Your name be held holy)

"Hallowed" is a difficult word to understand, especially for us in the west. In Greek, the root word for hallowed is *hagios,* which means "different." It is used in places such as the Jewish temple. The temple, priests, and the sabbath was all *hagios,* not like other places, people, or days. This part of the prayer means that God's name is to be treated differently from any other name. God's name is unique and is never to be treated in any other way. Hallowed reminds us of the commandment, "Do not take the Lord's name in vain."

God's name is not simply what He is called. His name means His character. All that He is and stands for is bound up in His name. Psalm 9:10 gives the classic meaning of hallowed: those who know God's name—who understand His nature and character— know that they can trust Him completely (See also Psalm 20:7). So, Lord, anchor us in the unique nature and character your name deserves.

The meaning of hallowed becomes even more evident when we note that God (and His name) is to be reverenced. Reverence carries these meanings:

1. Hebrews 13:6b "...he that comes to God must believe that He is..." There would never be any motivation or effort to know God unless there was a belief that He exists. One has no reason to reverence something that does not exist. So, the starting point for hallowing the Name of God (and reverencing it) is believing He exists.

   Upon discovery, every previously unknown people group was found to have an intuitive belief in a supreme being. Who that being is, what he is like, how one approaches him, etc., may not be clear, but God does exist. Even after the fall, the shadow of God remains in every person. Much more faith is required not to believe that God exists than to believe He does. Just think about how sensible it is to believe in the Creator.

   Suppose a person found a watch, something they had never seen or heard of before. Curious, they carefully examine it. Over time, they observe that the hands move around the dial with consistency and precision. Still curious, they open the watch's back and observe the amazing array of connected parts.

Their conclusion:

- Those parts created themselves out of various elements.
- They shaped themselves into unique and intricate shapes and designs.
- Somehow, they designed their individual shapes and designs to fit perfectly together.
- Somehow each part found its way to the workbench.
- On the workbench, each part attached itself to the other parts precisely so that each part worked in perfect unison.
- Having created and assembled themselves in perfect harmony, they activated themselves so that they marked the passing of time perfectly.
- Having done all of this, all the parts have sustained their functioning in perpetuity.

It makes perfect sense, doesn't it. NOT! There is a watch—a finished product—there must be a watchmaker. I came from somewhere, but where? Since I'm here, there has to be an explanation. Oh, yes, I came from my parents. And where did my parents come from? From their parents. And theirs? Ultimately, we must arrive at the beginning of life. Where did the first human beings come from? From the insane "the watch created itself" theory? We have permission to manage the created things in some ways, but we don't have the option to create the original. I reverence the God who was, is, and forever will be!

2. It is possible to acknowledge God as Creator and still not reverence Him. Reverence for Him requires engagement on His terms. Amazingly "...and He is a rewarder of those who diligently seek Him" (Hebrews 13:6c). God is a rewarder. He could be anything; He is God. He chooses to reward those who diligently seek Him. I'm moved to reverence such a God, every day, everywhere, in all places. I never want to be out of His presence. How foolish to know He exists and fail to abide in such a One as He is.

3. This brings us to a final thought on hallowing God's name. To hallow His name, we acknowledge His existence, His desire to engage us, fellowship us, and include us in His kingdom work, and... we surrender to Him and obey Him in all of our ways, all of the time. This third quality of hallowing/reverencing God is not burdensome or chaffing. It is a joy—pure, simple joy. There is no more incredible privilege than to be one of His, on mission with Him throughout the earth. Hallowed by Thy name!

What does Jesus want me to know?

Why does He want me to know this?

What does He want me to do in response?

Day Twenty-Five

"...Thy kingdom come, Thy will be done on
earth as it is in heaven..."

MATTHEW 6:10

Three things are necessary for a kingdom to exist: a king, a realm he rules, and subjects. Each of these three factors is included in Matthew 6:10. This is easier to understand when we approach the word from the Jewish perspective. Jewish (Hebrew) expression usually occurs in parallelisms. This is quite clear in the Psalms. The first part of a verse is repeated and amplified in the succeeding reference.

"The Lord is my shepherd—I shall not want." Psalm 23:1

"God is our refuge and strength—a very present help in time of trouble." Psalm 46:7

In the Model Prayer reference (6:10), Jesus says, "Thy kingdom come—Thy will be done on earth as it is being done in heaven." So, the kingdom of God (the King) is a domain on earth where His subjects [disciples] are to effectively carry out His will just like it is being done in heaven. In this sense—the work of God being done on earth as it is being done in heaven—involves the past, present, and future. At whatever time in history, disciples were doing the will of God on earth; they were/are in the kingdom.

To pray "...Thy will be done on earth as it is done in heaven" means that I, at all times, reverence His name and submit entirely to His will all day, every day. How we pray that prayer is vital

1. It could be prayed, oddly enough, grudgingly. "I guess I have no real choice since God is God...I have to do this. It's my duty; I have no option. Is it then really a prayer? No.

2. This prayer is to be prayed with an "I get to" attitude. When that is the disciple's attitude, one can be assured of God's love actively supporting and engaging him as he proceeds through the day. One can also depend on God's wisdom to deal with the issues that pop up.

It just makes sense to pray, "Thy will be done." Wouldn't God give His very best to his disciple who genuinely, joyfully approaches each day with an eagerness to partner with God in advancing the kingdom? What an adventure.

What does Jesus want me to know?

Why does He want me to know this?

What does He want me to do in response?

Day Twenty-Six

"Give us this day our daily bread..."

MATTHEW 6:11

As we have searched out some of its meaning so far, this prayer starts in the right place—with God, our Father. So far, it is designed to align us with Him. To the degree that we understand who He is, what He is like, and how He wills things to be—and we joyfully obey—we are aligned with Him as partners in advancing His kingdom on earth. To sustain our partnership, we human beings have particular needs.

"**Give** us our daily bread," reminds us the very staff of life is a gift. True, bread on the table is put there by the sweat of our face, but if God did not create grain with life in it, there would be no grain from which to make bread. It is as basic as that. We are reminded every day that life is a gift given by the Perfect infinite being in whom all things have their source, support, and end. Prayer, like faith, is dead without work. Without God, we are and can do nothing. Without our obedience, He can do nothing for us.

"Give **us** our daily bread..." shows it is not about me; it is about us. Prayer is unselfish. God displays His character in love by using us to share with others. To us who have a bit more than we need comes the privilege of sharing with those less fortunate. When "extra" comes, our first thought is for those who might be blessed in their legitimate need. Alas, extra is often wasted on frivolous "stuff," and the joy of being a blessing is lost forever.

"Give us **this day**..." reminds us it is one day at a time—that is all we have. Therefore, we only need bread for the day. God is not in the "storage building" business. Worry and anxiety over some distant concern can be avoided when we accept that our Good Father meets our daily needs. Just as He did in the wilderness with the manna, He meets our needs. We walk by faith. Faith, that when a need appears, there will be a supply for the need...then, not before. Manna was good for one day. Each day, fresh manna appeared. Stored manna, stunk (Exodus 16:1-21).

So, the prayer now focuses on God's awareness that we live in a physical body that must have provision. This phrase in the prayer is understood as a simple, straightforward acknowledgment that we need food, and the provision of that food involves God and us working together.

We are reminded that all of life is going, not knowing. Abraham first illustrated this. Hebrews 11 gives us snapshots of those who walked one day at a time with God. An ancient papyrus fragment contained Matthew's word for "daily"—*epiousios*. It was on a grocery shopping list. A lady was going to market with her list for *epiousios*...her daily bread.

What does Jesus want me to know?

Why does He want me to know this?

What does He want me to do in response?

Day Twenty-Seven

"Forgive us our debts, as we forgive our debtors."

MATTHEW 6:12

As food is indispensable to sustain physical life, forgiveness is indispensable for relational life. To forgive—*aphiemi*—means to release, remit, or send away. It is to write "paid in full" on the debt owed. It is by paying our sin debt that Jesus can write across our outstanding sin debt, "paid in full." By this forgiveness, we are brought into an eternal relationship with God. Furthermore, by forgiveness, fellowship is gained and maintained with both God and man.

"Relationship" is blood-based. By His shed blood to secure our release from sin, Jesus provided our blood-based standing with God. We are bonded by God to divine DNA. Once forgiven based on Jesus' finished work, we are God's child. Period. Just as a DNA test will prove that we are the child of our birth parents, so the born-again one is forever God's child. Nothing can change either human or divine relationships.

"Fellowship" is another matter that relates directly to "...forgive us..." Fellowship has to do with how we get along. In every human family, there is conflict, disobedience, sin. When that occurs, the issue is one of fellowship, not relationship. Every family has some means by which they deal with broken fellowship. Often efforts to deal with the issues are unhealthy, unwise, or simply wrong. ("You tell your sister that you are sorry" rarely restores fellowship between siblings because the offender's heart is not in it.)

In God's family, fellowship issues are effectively addressed on God's clear terms. God forgives when one of His children sins and expresses genuine repentance and confession. The result: the sin is remembered (by God) no more (I John 1:9). These are God's terms for gaining and sustaining fellowship for every Christian for every sin, every time.

"Forgive us our debts (trespasses)..." A debt *opheilemia* is accumulated obligations that exist and are past due. A debt relates to anything owed to another, not just money. Metaphorically, debt refers to sin. "Forgive our sins against others as God forgives us our sins."

Sin is such an ugly word. We don't like it. Mistakes, maybe, but sin? I agree that murderers, rapists, and people like that are sinners, but me? I know I'm not perfect (really?!), but the *sinner* is a little harsh. I've not been in jail, had my name in the headlines for a crime, been a defendant in a court of law. "Sin" is not a word that applies to me. Well, let's see. Five different words are used for "sin" in the New Testament.

1. The most common word for sin is *harmartia*. The word means "to miss the mark (bulls eye, target, standard.) It means to miss what could have been. Sadly, many people have three stages in life: I will be something, I might be something, I should have been something. The promise was never fulfilled. Are we as good as we could be? Am I *really*

doing my best? In truth, all of us fall short of our potential and God's standard. Sin.

2. *Opheilema* is the second word for sin in the New Testament. It means a failure to pay that which is due. None of us can say we have paid all that is due. There is always more that has not been done. We are not perfect.

3. It is a sin to know what is right but to do wrong anyway. One knows the law but breaks it anyway. *Anomia* is the word for this lawlessness. Can anyone say they have kept the Ten Commandments, much less the spirit of them? No, none.

4. There is a line between right and wrong. To know where that line is and what it means—and deliberately step over it is *parabasis:* Sin.

5. *Paraptoma* relates to the sin of the slippery slope. It is not as deliberate as *parabasis,* but it is putting ourselves again and again into positions or situations which lead to being swept away into sinfulness. You play with fire; sooner or later, you will get burned. You flirt often enough, and immorality will soon follow.

Most sin is not murder, rape, or headline news. Sin is most often subtle, secretive, of the heart. It starts there. Maybe the act of physical adultery never occurs, but oh, the times one has wished they could or has fantasized about it. Sin, Jesus said. Do not murder, but gossip, character assassination by hint or innuendo is a form of murder. Smile, "I'm so happy for you (but I wish it were mine, not yours.")

Blessed is the person who realizes and acknowledges their sin. Blessed is the person who makes no excuses but calls sin what God calls it. Blessed is the person who quickly and completely deals with his public and private sins according to God's standards. Blessed is the person who realizes the frightening consequences if they refuse to forgive others.

We stay with the forgiveness thought and connect verses 14-15 to verse 12 before proceeding to verse 13. Why is it so frightening to not forgive another? Jesus is very clear. You will be forgiven in proportion to how you forgive others. You decide. How much do you want to be forgiven? If you don't forgive others "just as God has forgiven you"— you are asking God not to forgive you. Is that really what you want? There is no wiggle room here. Jesus meant what He said.

If one comes to God asking forgiveness knowing there is an unaddressed breach in fellowship with another brother, there is no forgiveness from God. No response will come from God until the broken human fellowship breach is dealt with according to His teaching in Matthew 5 and 18. In this matter, you don't deal with God first; you deal with your brother first. If fellowship with a fellow-believer is unresolved, it is an automatic issue with God, and He will not hear you (Psalm 66:18; Proverbs 28:13). I John 1:9 begins with the word "If..." meaning that **if** we confess our sin...He is faithful and just to forgive, but there is no forgiveness if we don't confess.

Someone says, "I will forgive, but I will not forget." Jesus never required forgetting as a condition of forgiving. Forgiveness is a choice to remit, release (to God) whatever offense has occurred. Anything of consequence will likely be remembered. That is not the issue. The issue is: what happens to you when you remember. God forgives when an offender genuinely regrets that the offense occurred and repents of his sin. Such regret is accompanied by a determination that no such sin will occur again. However, if you remember the offense with resentment or anger, you have not forgiven.

With forgiveness of an offense—even if it is remembered—comes love, *agape* love. There is no bitterness or desire for revenge. If you learned of a legitimate need your former offender now has, wouldn't you want to respond to that need, if possible? Isn't that the way God deals with our offenses?

What does Jesus want me to know?

Why does He want me to know this?

What does He want me to do in response?

Day Twenty-Eight

"...lead us not into temptation"

MATTHEW 6:13

The word temptation (*peirazein*) almost always means "to entice to evil." Originally it meant "to test." The outcome of temptation was intended to be positive. As a result of the test, one was intended to be stronger and more equipped for the intended purpose. Examples include Abraham's test with offering Isaac as a sacrifice (Genesis 22:1). Jesus being led by the Spirit into the wilderness to face Satan (Matthew 4:1) is another example.

God is in the testing business, not the "enticing to sin" business. James deals with the difference between testing and enticing to evil in James 1. No Christian advances in maturity without testing. Every test is God-designed to strengthen, refine and improve the Christian. Tests take many forms. One of the ways God may use to mature us could involve Satan. He is under God's control, and God sometimes uses him. Job is a classic example. Since Satan may be used to test us, let's take a brief look at him.

The Bible never considers Satan in the abstract or an idea or force. He is a person, a being. "Satan" means adversary, one who opposes.

The identity of Satan grew to mean "one who pleads a case against" another. From there, Satan can mean not just an opponent who prosecutes but one who will do whatever is necessary to defeat. "*Diabolus*" means a slanderer and is a word used for Satan, the devil. Satan is who opposes every Christian in any and every way possible. He is extremely cunning and patient. He is constantly probing, prowling about seeking an entrance and opportunity to entice one to evil.

What is Satan looking for in us? He is particularly interested in the very thing that caused him to fall—pride. His original dealing with a human being began in the Garden of Eden with an implied question: Is God good? Eve was tempted to question why a good God would withhold fruit from the Tree of Knowledge of Good and Evil.

Satan's original and current strategy focuses on three things (I John 2:16), at least one of which is effective against every human being:

1. Self-ism – The desire to be recognized...in the spotlight

2. Sensual-ism – A sensual lifestyle ...gratifying/satisfying the senses, especially the sexual

3. Stuff-ism – The unbridled pursuit of things... materialism, "stuff."

Satan will use anything and anyone to destroy a Christian. Satan can just stand by and watch us be our own worst enemies in many instances. Somehow drawn time after time into the same foolish, destructive practices as James said (1:14), we have no one to blame but ourselves.

The insatiable search for gratification is a second vulnerability Satan uses. Paul describes the practices of those driven by the "...lusts of their hearts" (Romans 1:24). The never-enough effort to satisfy this appetite is described in the verses following and are so despicable we can hardly read them. This unending drive cannot contain itself and, in the end, makes a final effort to find satisfaction by recruiting others to share in the indescribable debauchery by which they live (Romans 1:32).

Then, Satan ceaselessly creates new "apples" to dabble before our lustful eyes. Endless streams of glitzy new products, meticulously researched and crowd-tested, bombard us day after day. Closets fill, garages are stuffed. Duplication's pile up. Give it to charity; throw it into the dumpster. Buy, buy! It's a never-ending cycle of spending money we don't have for things we don't need to impress people we don't ever know.

Then, some people have an agenda for us (not bad within itself), but it may tempt us to forsake God's call for another life choice. W. A. Criswell—for nearly fifty years, pastor of the First Baptist Church of Dallas—faced such temptation from his well-meaning mother. She was determined he would be a medical doctor. He had to work very hard to overcome her temptation and remain faithful to God's calling. Blessed is the person who has the maturity to discern who and what would derail them from the road to becoming all that God saved them to be.[21]

Beyond these fundamental tools of Satan, there is the temptation that arises within our strengths–"I would never." Pride, Satan loves it! Blessed is the person who, informed, can pray:

Father,

You know through and through. I pray You will both make me aware and be my strength with the testing time comes today. Don't allow me to get in over my head so that I yield to the enticement to sin. Deliver me from the cunning of the evil one. For the honor of Your name and the integrity of my witness, lead me not into temptation, for I have no confidence in my ability to pass the test alone.

What does Jesus want me to know?

Why does He want me to know this?

What does He want me to do in response?

Day Twenty-Nine

"Moreover, when you fast, do not be like the hypocrites, with a sad countenance. For they disfigure their faces that they may appear to men to be fasting. Assuredly I say to you, they have their reward. But you, when you fast, anoint your head and wash your face, so that you do not appear to men to be fasting but to your Father who is in the secret place: and your Father who sees in secret will reward you openly...." (Not "if" but "when")

MATTHEW 6:16-18

Fasting (*nesteno*) "to abstain from food" is an ancient practice of Muslim and Jewish faiths. Both religions follow similar practices. Only one day of fasting was mandatory for the Jew, the Day of Atonement (Leviticus 16:31). The Jews, however, determined there were other reasons to fast.

1. Moses (Exodus 24:15), Daniel (Daniel 9:3), even Jesus (Matthew 4:2) all fasted. In those cases, fasting was preparing for a revelation, for insight, and strength from the Father,

2. Fasting was called for when there was a need for national repentance. Judges 20:26 and Nehemiah 9:1 are examples.

Perhaps the National Day of Prayer is a modern-day example in America.

3. Individually, fasting was used, especially by the Pharisees to get God's attention or approval.

As He did with His teaching on almsgiving and prayer, Jesus addressed the subject of fasting. He condemned the common hypocritical practices on the same basis as with the previous two practices among the Pharisees—the to-be-see-by-men, which He soundly condemned. The following were some of the practices followed in fasting by those seeking the approval and applause of men.

1. They chose days when Jerusalem was most crowded to put on their fasting performance. The more who could see their apparent piety, the better.

2. They carefully prepared so that their appearance made the fast they were doing the most obvious. Unkempt clothing, messy hair, cosmetics of various kinds to make their faces seem paler were some practices. So, these rather weird-looking ones stalked their way through the crowds, wild hair, soiled, disheveled clothing, and hypocritical, one and all.

The wisest rabbis condemned these practices as vehemently as Jesus did. Fasting for the sake of ostentatious piety is useless and a mockery of its real purpose. There are several benefits to fasting, although few in America give fasting any thought. Fasting is a worthy practice for these reasons:

1. It is good for health when wisely practiced. Just as trash accumulates unless properly and effectively disposed of,

excessive calories amount to the build-up of "trash" (excessive weight) in the human body.

2. It is a good test of self-control. What can we not do without? If we can't do without any specific thing, we are enslaved to it. Christians rightly condemn alcoholism, smoking, promiscuity, etc., but we easily excuse enslavement to food or the need to control, for example. Periodic testing of any habit or desire is wise.

3. Fasting from any practice helps us appreciate that practice more afterward. Familiarity breeds contempt is an ancient understatement that has some validity. Fasting helps deflate the entitlement mentality.

4. The most important reason for fasting is the intentional, private commitment to know God more intimately. To forgo the time required for the preparation, indulgence, and clean-up after a meal to devote that time to a humble, genuine time with God has many benefits. As with praying and giving, fasting is between the believer and God.

Jesus affirmed and encouraged fasting. He did it Himself. Blessed is the Christian who, simply for the joy of knowing God more intimately, deliberately chooses periods of fasting. This teaching on fasting concludes Jesus' teaching on the three great areas of Christian practice. Charitable giving, prayer, and fasting are practices Jesus strongly advocated while strongly condemning the hypocritical practice of all three.

His principles by which the greatest, eternal good may come from the proper practice of these three aspects of the Christian lifestyle are timeless. There is no greater threat than that which is more concerned for our comfort than for our character. Blessed is the person who has ears to hear. As we shall see in the following body of instruction, Jesus enlarges upon the eternal implications of these practices for the disciple.

What does Jesus want me to know?

Why does He want me to know this?

What does He want me to do in response?

Day Thirty

"Do not lay up for yourselves treasures on earth, where moth and rust destroy and where thieves break through and steal; but lay up for yourselves treasures in heaven, where neither moth nor rust destroys and where thieves do not break in and steal. For where your treasure is, there your heart will be also."

MATTHEW 6:19-21

How great a challenge this section of Jesus' teaching has for the American Christian! Every year during the Christmas season, we watch a repeating cycle. Stores overflow with—for the most part—shoddy merchandise, which will be broken, obsolete, and abandoned by next Christmas. Impulse buying abounds. "I've just got to have it" items lose their shine and appeal in a few weeks. Our garages and expensive storage spaces are filled with stuff. Still, we want more. Each Christmas—any Christmas in the West—the greatest challenge is to find something for someone they don't already have. If I sound cynical, perhaps I am, but Jesus takes up this insatiable quest for more—more that relates only to the brief time we have on earth. Forgotten is the message of that small poster on my grandmother's bedroom wall:

"Only one life...'twill soon be past,

Only what's done for Christ will last."

This is not just a modern madness. Humankind has always been prone to impulse. This includes both the quantity and quality of things. Both material and relational decisions are most commonly made not on a thoughtful, prayerful basis but the impulse of the moment based on a desire.

The Jews had three primary sources of wealth: clothing, money, and grain. Much time and effort were given to accumulating them. Each of these three has a natural enemy. By definition, each of these is quite valuable and could easily be lost. Jesus taught that wise ones gain a clear perspective on these three basic things. He did not oppose them. He did condemn their being the focus of life. He taught how these three things can be used in time to enhance treasure in eternity.

Clothing was highly valued in Palestine. Gehazi (II Kings 5:22) and Achan (Joshua 7:21) illustrate how clothing was viewed. Clothing in Palestine with the most value was made of wool. Cotton and linen clothing were more commonly worn. The natural enemy of clothing, especially woolen clothing, was the moth. (By the way, moths live on less than any other creature...they eat holes.) The other natural enemy of clothes is thieves.

A man goes to great expense to secure an impressive wardrobe only to discover that moths had destroyed it or thieves had dug through the flimsy clay walls of the house and stolen it. The only thing of value the man had was gone.

A man buries his coins in a safe place. Burial in a secret location was thought to be the safest way to keep coins from being stolen. One day, the man needs to purchase a piece of property. He quietly goes to his secret place and digs up his bag of coins. Coins of the day were very subject to rusting, especially when in contact with moisture. To his dismay, his coins are now a pile of rust. His wealth is gone. The work of a lifetime is lost.

Grain provided for bread, the heart of every meal. Without grain, the society of the day was in great danger. Many Old Testament stories relate to the presence or absence of grain. The whole Exodus narrative originated in a famine and the quest for grain. Stored grain sustained them when the uncertainty of weather and pestilence struck in Palestine. The natural enemy of grain is thieves and vermin. Then, as in many third-world countries today, almost as much grain is lost by spoilage, rats and mice, or theft as is consumed by the hungry. Grain was a valued yet vulnerable source of wealth.

So, what did Jesus teach about these three things the people of the day pursued? He did not condemn any of the three sources of wealth. He condemned the attitude of those who made "stuff" the central focus of their life and how people used their possessions.

In contrast to these this-world-only practices, Jesus teaches on where true, eternal value is found. The underlying principle Jesus emphasized was, "take the long look." Perhaps in a time of fasting, the Lord refocuses your perspective. To what end are you so driven? Does stuff satisfy you? The more you have, the greater your worry over preserving, protecting, and using it. Every day is focused on gaining more stuff and safeguarding what you have. For what? Does such a focus and drive leave you any time to live? You are going to die. Then what? Who will all this stuff belong to then? What will they do with your stuff? Usually, they fight over it until it is all gone. Now, that's a life worth living, isn't it!?

What is most striking about what Jesus taught about wealth is how obvious it is. If anyone took a simple, common-sense look at the whole subject of possessions and how to use them, much grief would be avoided. Just think about the common sense Jesus makes.

1. Possessions never satisfy the deepest needs and desires of the heart. The desire for peace and satisfaction seems to be universal. "If I had that...or them...or...I would be content." NOT. When one breaks through the veneer of stuff to the heart, who has ever found a contented person? Who has found rest because of their stuff? Nobody.

2. Possessions are a constant worry. The wealthy are besieged by those seeking a handout. Lottery winners suddenly find long-lost relatives or persons who feel somehow entitled to some of the winnings. Scam artists seek to get the lottery winner to invest with them in crooked schemes. Money brings out the worst in people, including their own families. Through over fifty years of dealing directly (often very personally) with people, I have found that where money is involved, the worst in people is what comes out...not the best.

3. Possessions provide an almost impossible challenge to one's character. With money, who has to be concerned about anything? If one gets into trouble and gets caught, a bribe or some hush money will take care of it. With money, one doesn't have to worry about doing what is right, just because it is right. This may be true in the short term, but Jesus is teaching (as Paul later applied it): "Be not deceived GOD is not mocked..."

4. Everyone dies. What will happen to the stuff then which was so important? If—as is almost always not the case—wealth has been used for great projects, to endow great universities, or to build political dynasties, what happens when those who provided such investments are gone? Their contribution may be remembered for a few years. Then nobody cares. Besides, whatever our money has purchased will be good only to feed the flames, which will destroy everything in the end anyway. Jesus addressed all of this. Yes, everyone dies, but nobody ceases to exist. What about the next life? What will the next life be like? Jesus said the answer depends greatly on what one does with the possessions they are allowed to handle on earth.

In the wisdom of God, people are allowed to manage certain possessions. One can invest those possessions on earth to gain an earthly reward. Many profit from such investments to a certain extent. Others invest their possessions to profit in the life to come after death. Invest your wealth here on earth, and it's gone when you are. Invest in things eternal, and you have it forever. Be content with food and shelter; invest the rest in things eternal is what Jesus taught. Again, how simple and sensible.

How tragic is the typical story? A man does well financially. He uses his possessions well. He is respected and appreciated for his character and his generosity. His whole life is honorably spent. His estate is large and well invested. Though commendable, all of this is for this life only. His estate is left to his children. Before the will can be probated, the fight has begun. In the end, lawyers have most of the estate, and all that the man spent a lifetime to accumulate is a hollow shadow if it exists at all. How wise it would be if that estate had been so designed to ensure that God's kingdom would be the beneficiary.

Truer words were never spoken: Your heart will be where your treasure is. If the only thing one values are on earth, his heart will have no interest in the world to come. If one's heart is set on eternity, all things will be held loosely. If one's great wealth is what makes his life worth living, he will find it difficult to die. Fix your eyes on that which will never cease. In focusing your life on things eternal and investing there, you will never be sorry, Jesus taught.

What does Jesus want me to know?

Why does He want me to know this?

What does He want me to do in response?

Day Thirty-One

"The lamp of the body is the eye if therefore your eye is good your whole body will be full of light but if your eye is bad your whole body will be full of darkness. If, therefore, the light that is in you is darkness how great is that darkness."

MATTHEW 6:22-23

Windows let light into the room. The condition of the window affects the quality and quantity of light. The eye is the entry point for light into the body. No other body part serves this purpose. The condition of the eye determines the amount and quality of light. I found this true when I had cataract surgery. Eyes that are diseased or damaged limit the light. Another way to understand these verses is to see the symbolic meaning of the eye/light subject.

What does the eye "being single" mean? What is the "evil" eye? The Greek helps us. The literal meaning of these two words (single and evil) is the focus of Greek. As always, these words are connected to what Jesus has been teaching in the Sermon on the Mount.

"Single" is *haplous,* and the corresponding noun form is *haplotes.* These words are often used in the New Testament, and they mean a spirit of generosity. "Single" means generous. James says God gives liberally (James 1:5). Paul urged the Romans to give with a generous spirit (Romans 12:8). Paul reminded the church in Corinth of the generosity of the Macedonian churches (II Corinthians 9:11). Connecting this generous spirit to His teaching on possessions and how to view them, we see the continuity of Jesus' teaching. It is the person who "sees" the condition of another and is instantly inclined to respond generously that Jesus commends.

Then, there is the evil eye. The light that flows into the soul of a diseased/distorted person is dim and limited, even darkened. The Greek word for the evil eye is *ponerous,* and it means: grudging, reluctant to the point of denial. The evil eye can see (or admit) no reason to respond to the need of another person...just themselves.

Deuteronomy 15:9 addresses this grudging, denying spirit in practice in the Jewish culture whereby all debts were forgiven every seven years. The person with an "evil" eye might deny a request for a loan if the seventh year were near, lest the one borrowing uses the seventh-year forgiveness clause and never repay the loan. Such a calculation is the opposite of the generous spirit which trusts God to put all things in proper order.

Proverbs 23:6 and 28:22 urges one not to sit at the table of a host who resents every bite you take. Nothing provides a clear, undistorted view of life and people like generosity. Nothing so prejudices an outlook on life as a grudging, resentful spirit. Generosity sees the best; grudging sees the worst. Both are automatic.

The generous person lives out Paul's teaching to the Galatians (Galatians 6:10). Such a person uses every opportunity to do good to/for whoever needs it and finds peace and satisfaction within themselves. The evil person knows nothing of this joy. How great is the darkness of the self-centered person?

What does Jesus want me to know?

Why does He want me to know this?

What does He want me to do in response?

Day Thirty-Two

*"No man can serve two masters for either he will hate the
one and love the other or else he will be loyal to one and
despise the other you cannot serve God and mammon."*

MATTHEW 6:24

Every person has a god. Every person becomes like the god they
serve. The keyword in this verse is "serve" *douleuo,* which means to
be enslaved. The slave was a thing in the ancient world. He had no
rights,no voice, no protection. He was completely owned and used
by his owner at the owner's pleasure. This was true all the time, 24/7.
Never at any time did the slave have any freedom.

Jesus is saying the believer is bought and paid for. Every Christian is
owned entirely by the Lord. Indeed, we have no will nor time apart
from Him. A Christian cannot say, "Most of who/what I am belongs
to God alone, but some of whom/what I am is by my choice."
The Christian cannot assume that some of life is "Christian," and
some is secular. One is all in...or not. There's no other choice, and
those who live like they are semi-slaves know only frustration and
dissatisfaction...a condition most of us are all too familiar with.

Any serious Christian recognizes the validity of the concept Jesus is emphasizing here. We get it, theoretically. We are to understand and practice this literally. It is in the application/practice of the truth that we struggle. It is the process of sanctification that moves one along from part Him/part me toward becoming a *dulos*, a slave of Jesus Christ. Christians who commit themselves to the Holy Spirit's transforming work find that to be enslaved to Jesus is the most liberating condition possible. To be partially committed in continuous frustration and disappointment. No person is more miserable than the carnal Christian. No person is more dangerous than one who is actively engaged in resisting the *dulos* role. Ask Jonah about that.

Jesus reemphasizes this thought by restating it: you cannot be enslaved to God and mammon. One or the other will win. Sadly, mammon almost always wins. What is mammon? Originally it meant possessions—that which a person had. Then, mammon evolved into meaning "to entrust." One entrusted his possessions to another for safekeeping—a safety deposit box at the bank. Then it developed further, and became mammon: that in which a person puts their trust. Mammon became those material possessions that a person trusted for their well-being and security.

Three great principles form the basis for understanding the role of possessions in the Christian life. Possessions are never a problem. The Bible tells us of many who were wealthy. An abundance can be a great benefit to both the possessor and those they might serve with their wealth. It is the <u>use</u> of possessions that Jesus addresses. According to Jesus, this is the role of possessions for the Christian:

1. Possessions are gifts from God. In His generosity, God allows the Christian to handle, and to some degree to alter or

rearrange possessions. In the end, that is all a person can do. He can never say, "This is mine to do with as I please." Psalm 24:1; 50:1-2 refers to God's sole ownership of everything on earth. This includes our abilities, which are also gifts of God (Matthew 25:15).

Malachi writes of the person who robs God. The word for "rob" means to embezzle. A robber takes what he has no right to touch. An embezzler is one the owner trusts to handle the owner's money. But in managing the money, which he has every right to do, he steals some of it and says it is his. Acting as if possessions belong to himself, the Christian violates the first of Jesus' great principles regarding possessions when he embezzles.

2. Possessions are important, but people are far more important. Those hearing Jesus teach were well-acquainted with the awful scourge of slavery and the treatment of slaves as living tools. Not so long ago, even, children were enslaved to work the factories and mines of wealthy men. Conditions were horrible for the children. They were living tools to be used for greater riches for heartless men. Thankfully, child labor laws ended that practice. Human trafficking is an even more despicable, worldwide trade in modern times. Children figure prominently as the victims of this horrible commerce. The depraved lusts of men are the source of this market. The love of money drives those who seek to satisfy the darkest beastly cravings of men.

3. Possessions are meant to enrich the best elements of life. Used to relieve human misery, lift rather than destroy, and prioritize the eternal, possessions are an unspeakable blessing.

When possessions are used as if God does not exist, the result is a great loss both in time and money.

4. There is a way to live so that what one is entrusted with is a way to bless. When possessions are used for eternal good, joy and reward are waiting in the life to come. Jesus said, "It is more blessed to give than to receive" (Acts 20:35). Blessed is the person who uses what God puts in their trust to enhance and enrich others.

What does Jesus want me to know?

Why does He want me to know this?

What does He want me to do in response?

Day Thirty-Three

"Therefore I say to you, do not worry about your life, what you will eat or what you will drink; nor about your body, what you will put on. Is not life more than food and the body more than clothing? Look at the birds of the air for they neither sow nor reap nor gather into barns, yet your heavenly Father feeds them. Are you not of more value than they? Which of you by worrying can add one cubit to his stature? So why do you worry about clothing?

Consider the lilies of the field, how they grow; they neither toil nor spin; and yet I say to you that even Solomon in all his glory was not arrayed like one of these. Now if God so clothes the grass of the field, which today is, and tomorrow is thrown into the oven, will he not much more clothe you, O you of little faith? Therefore, do not worry saying, what shall we eat? Or what shall we drink? Or what shall we wear? For after all these things the Gentiles seek.

For your heavenly Father knows that you need all these things. But seek first the kingdom of God and his righteousness, and all these things shall be added to you. Therefore, do not worry about tomorrow, for tomorrow will worry about its things. Sufficient for the day is its trouble."

MATTHEW 6:25-34

Here is that tremendous connecting word: "therefore." When we read that word, we pause to ask: "What is the word there for?" It is there to arrest our thinking, to urge us to reflect and draw a proper conclusion on what has just been said. All that Jesus just taught in the entire Sermon on the Mount is included in "therefore." However, the concept of possessions is meant in particular.

As usual, Jesus examines two sides of one coin in this text. On one side, He forbids something and on the other side commands something. The central thought is about worry. *Merimnan* is the word. It means a life filled with stressful, anxious care.

"Take no thought" does not mean one is to live blindly, recklessly, thoughtlessly, make-no-plans-for-the-future. It means to meet life with prudence and serenity. Plan ahead wisely. Be responsible for handling resources, knowing that some periods are more productive than others. Balance your life with responsibility on the one hand, and trust in God on the other hand.

The rabbis said to teach a son a trade; because if you don't, you teach him to steal. The wise man has found the balance between two extremes. In this text, Jesus presents five factors related to worry:

1. He begins by reminding us that everything we are and have is a gift. He starts with the greatest gift: life. Our very life is a gift from God. Having given us life, He gives us a body to live in. Wouldn't He provide for the house He gave us to live in? Of course, He would! He thought it all out. Giving us life, He has already planned everything that will ever come to us. We can trust Him to have it ready when we need it. He neither tells us all that is to come nor does He weigh us down with huge resources to manage before we need those

resources—one day at a time. Nothing is provided before it is required. Manna was provided each morning except for the Sabbath. The Sabbath was the only time manna could be stored As always, it is both one day at a time, and store up prudently.

2. Nature declares the glory of God. Animals work hard for their daily bread, but they don't worry. Bears store up extra fat only when a period of scarcity is before them (hibernation). Birds are wise to recognize where their daily bread might come from. I have watched birds sit in pecan trees and wait for a car to come by and crack the pecans on the street. I sat beside the drive-through window of a fast-food place and watched God deliver a well-rounded meal to a bird who sat on the curb and waited for the next car. When a car stopped at the window, the bird hopped on the bumper and checked out the cafeteria in the car grille. Daily bread in a variety of flavors... delivered!

3. Don't worry. Just use some common sense. No person can, by worry, add the slightest to their height. God designed our body and knows how one's body is to be cared for. Stress and anxiety (worry) add nothing. It usually has the opposite effect. We are genetically wired. Make the best of what God gave you. Live a healthy lifestyle and leave the rest to God. Worry is pointless.

4. When a clay oven needed to be heated quickly, the common practice was to kindle a fire of dried grass and flowers gathered from the countryside. Grass and flowers served a practical, if very brief, purpose. But brief as their life was, flowers were created as a thing of beauty. Why bother with making flowers

beautiful if they are only here briefly and then fuel a quick fire? It is just a quality of our Father to beautify all of His creation. The life of the ordinary person was enriched by the beauty and utility of the flower. Flowers display the glory of God; they do so without a single worry. They just BE. Learn from the flower.

5. The heathen lived in fear and anxiety, especially regarding their gods. Unknown and unknowable, capricious, vengeful and angry, these gods were reasons for the heathen to be anxious. But the Christian's God is none of these things. He is the opposite. Loving, faithful, engaged right alongside His children, He is trustworthy and unchangeable. He invites us into His presence. He has proved that without exception. What possible reason is there for not trusting God? None. Worry is distrust of God.

So, how does the Christian take in the wisdom of these five factors regarding worry? Jesus presents two ways to overcome the habit of worry.

1. Understand and accept God's will and way of living on earth (Matthew 6:10). He is here. He has plans for you (plans for good, always). Settle that in your mind and live faithfully. Everything will work out exactly right for you as you trust Him "...in all of your ways." Experience the good of that conviction and practice it one day at a time. Worry has no power when our focus is on God, His kingdom, and the remembrance of His trustworthiness. Keep a kingdom focus.

2. Live today. Live it well in keeping with all He has taught us. Through the day, pray for discernment as each experience/

decision confronts you. Pray first. Pray that God will align your response with His will for that which has come to your awareness. Then, having discerned God's will, pray for the courage to do what is right. Right, as God defines right. Rest there—no need to worry. Our faithful Father will make it all fit together for good. And, if you missed what He intended, He will faithfully—and gently—bring you back from the misdirection.

Now, let's summarize Jesus' teaching on worry:

1. Worry is needless, pointless, and harmful. It seeks to do the impossible and fails every time. Obviously, what is past is past. Worrying about it cannot change it. You can't un-ring the bell or unscramble the eggs, yet people live years regretting something or worrying about it. Repentance and obedience might redress a worry from the past, but worry won't. Sooner or later, you will have to abandon your hope of having a better past. Worrying about the future is equally foolish. "What if" cannot be answered. Study after study shows that almost none of the things people worry about ever happen.

2. Worry is a kind of amnesia. Somehow the faithfulness of God to deal with the issues of life is forgotten when a new storm arrives. All He has done in the past is predictive of what He will do with this present storm.

3. There may be greater sins, but none are more destructive than worry. Worry is destructive in both body and soul. It compounds physical ailments of all kinds. Worry destroys peace of mind. It is in every way destructive, in no way

constructive. Seek first God's kingdom and His righteousness, and all you need will be provided.

What does Jesus want me to know?

Why does He want me to know this?

What does He want me to do in response?

Day Thirty-Four

"Judge not, that you be not judged. For with what judgment you judge, you will be judged; and with the measure you use, it will be measured back to you. And why do you look at the speck in your brother's eye, but do not consider the plank in your own? Or how can you say to your brother, let me remove the speck from your eye; and look, a plant is in your eye? Hypocrite! First, remove the plank from your eye, and then you will see clearly to remove the speck from your brother's eye."

MATTHEW 7:1-5

The subject now changes, but the basic concept does not change: Understand and obey God's will and way in all matters. Take Him literally. Jesus has just taught on worry and the concepts which relate to it. Understanding and obeying God's provision for the needs of life allows a person to relax, trust, and forego worry.

Even though the subject is judging, the instruction is similar: understand the entire subject, then trust/obey God, and He will do the right thing at the right time in the right way...every time. He often uses one of His disciples to express His response to a need.

This is what the disciple needs to know about judging and being judgmental. The word for judge is *krino,* and it has several shades of meaning. It is essential to understand each shade.

To understand what Jesus taught in these verses, it is essential to work through the shades of meaning, which will help us understand the difference between "to judge" and "to be judgmental." The difference is often missed, which makes a huge difference in godly living.

God established the concept of authority, Himself. He did so to regulate society and His kingdom. He established four authority structures: government, business, family, and church. Each of these authority structures is necessary for a well-ordered society. All four are related and are beneficial. Violation of these authority structures destroys order and godly living.

In each authority system, someone has to determine if the system functions as God designed it. In other words, someone has to judge, consider, evaluate, conclude. This, they are to do wisely, based on God's design. Humbly taking all pertinent details into account, the one making the determination always does so, knowing that a Judge greater than himself will judge him. The judge is accountable to the Judge.

Unless there is a judge to wisely, thoroughly, humbly consider all the pertinent details in a case, no valid verdict can be reached. Without judges—those who function every day in many situations (attempting to do the right things as God defines "right")—the world would be in utter chaos. Jesus is not teaching that there should be no judges and judging. In fact, in His conclusion, He presents an opposite conclusion: *be sure that you judge*. Isn't there a contradiction here? No, as we shall see.

The meaning of Jesus' teaching becomes quite clear when we consider a related meaning to *krino*. Jesus is condemning judgmentalism. He condemns the common practice, then and now, to pass judgment on another based on ignorance, bias, and incomplete information. The critical, negative, and "superior" person decides about another person (and almost always shares that judgment with others). Such a judgmental person will never be helpful to the one being judged.

How badly the world needs judges. Judgmental judges so damage society. If I'm ever on trial in a court of law, I want a judge to preside—a judge who makes sure that the truth, the whole truth, and nothing but the truth is applied in my case. Furthermore, I want a judge who is just and makes sure the truth is the final determinant for both the accused and the accuser. I wouldn't want a judge who has made up their mind before the truth is ever presented. A judge, yes. Judgmental, no.

Jesus gives His reasons for the concept of judge/judgmental. Bottom line: someone has a problem—something in their eye. It hurts, limits, and needs to be taken care of. Now, who do you want to help you with your eye problem? Someone who has far more eye trouble than you have, or someone who can see clearly? The one with more eye trouble will never take care of you and your need. Moreover, they are going to cause you more pain if they try.

No, I want someone who knows what it is like to have something in the eye and has a lot of tenderness, care, and compassion when they seek to help me. Sooner or later, everybody gets something in their eye. Blessed is the person who has a judge when that happens—someone who carefully applies every "law" required to deliver you from your eye problem. Miserable is the person who has someone judgmental when such a problem arises.

See how much sense Jesus makes in His teaching? The rabbis recognized this. They had a saying, "God will favorably judge him who judges his neighbor favorably." Three great reasons are given for not being judgmental.

1. We never know the whole story of another's circumstance. People do what they do for a reason. Few ever know the load another carries. Therefore, don't be judgmental. You don't know.

2. There are no unbiased people. The Greeks sometimes conducted trials in the dark so that no one would see the defendant and be biased by what they saw. The American justice system is symbolized by a blindfolded lady holding a balance scale. Patience must be exercised.

3. Only God is wise and knowledgeable enough to pass judgment. Pay attention to your issues and failures. My Grandpa used to say, "I spend half my time taking care of my own business, and the other half leaving the other fellow's alone."

Yes, we are to commit to responding to every hurt to which God introduces us. Having learned of the need, we respond with humility, compassion, and *agape* love. We pray that such a one will be available to us in our time of need. In this way, all of us have a better hope for making the blessings of the Christian faith attractive to a lost world as well as being a faithful servant in our Christian family.

What does Jesus want me to know?

Why does He want me to know this?

What does He want me to do in response?

Day Thirty-Five

*"Do not give what is holy to the dogs; or cast your pearls
before swine, lest they trample them under their feet, and
turn and tear you in pieces."*

MATTHEW 7:6

In judging, one must be very careful and wise. Discernment, wisdom, and patience must be exercised. The early church was an island of godliness in a raging sea of religious ideology. Early Christians had a driving passion to see the whole world saved. The two-sided coin of the issue of spreading the gospel was this: The gospel is for all people just as they are—share it.

On the other side of the coin, the gospel must be preserved as unchanging truth. Christians, and their message, must always be available, but they must also sustain their purity. Unless the purity of the church membership is diligently preserved, Christianity will become just another religion in a world awash in competing religions.

In this verse, Jesus is requiring the Christian to be wise and discerning in sharing the gospel. When, where, and how to share the gospel is His subject. Why the concern? Some are so biased, callous, and depraved that anything related to the gospel is attacked, mocked, and slandered. Not only is there no interest in the gospel, but there is also a belligerent reaction to both the message and the messenger. Jesus warns Christians not to share the gospel where such attitudes exist. Isn't that a contradiction and betrayal of the Great Commission? No, it is simply good judgment.

What is the Christian to do then? Indeed, the Christian is not to be judgmental. The mocker certainly has a speck in his eye. To even have an opportunity to remove the speck so the belligerent one might see the beauty of the gospel, the Christian must be sure to live a clean life. It is not in blindly plunging ahead out of duty to share the gospel, so the belligerent one is won to Christ. It is the wise, when-the-time-is-right sharing that is effective.

Sooner or later, circumstances greater than the belligerent's questions and mockery will come, and with these circumstances, an openness to the gospel. Christian, pray God will engineer circumstances to cause the mocker to seek answers his mockery cannot supply. Then, an honest response to the gospel is most likely to be considered.

So, Christian, discern when to speak and when just to be. Share the gospel with every person who gives evidence that they will honestly consider the message. If you discern the Holy Spirit is at work, but the gospel will only bring greater reaction, simply be Christian, continue to pray, and wait.

What does Jesus want me to know?

Why does He want me to know this?

What does He want me to do in response?

Day Thirty-Six

"Ask and it will be given to you seek, and you will find; knock, and it will be open to you. For everyone who asks receives, and he who seeks finds, and to him who knocks, it will be opened. Or what man is there among you who, if his son asks for bread will give him a stone? Or if he asks for a fish, would he give him a serpent? If you then, being evil, know how to give good gifts to your children, how much more will your Father who is in heaven give good things to those who ask Him!"

MATTHEW 7:7-11

Few subjects are more frustrating in the Christian faith than prayer. All Christians agree prayer is central to the Christian life. But how, when, for what, how long are we to pray? What if I'm praying sincerely but wrongly? What conditions must I meet, if any, to pray effectively? What if I am just praying for what I want, not for what God wills? If God knows everything and will only respond according to His character, why pray—He's going to do what He's going to do? Right?

We learn much about prayer by studying Jesus' teaching in the Model Prayer. Here, we have some additional insight. I understand that prayer has certain preconditions if it is to be as God intends. The one praying needs to be fully persuaded:

1. God is the Originator of all prayer. All true prayer begins with God and is intended for one thing—to advance His kingdom.

2. Simply because He chooses to do so, God enlists His followers in a partnership by which He in heaven and His partners on earth join to advance His kingdom.

3. To be effective, God must be and do what He does; Christians must be and do what they are to do. The Christian is often tempted to reverse the roles and get God to do their will while seeking to do what only He can do. This is often unintentional but is true.

4. The Christian comes to God to pray with an attitude: "Thy will be done." Delighting and trusting in God for the joy of being a partner with God, the Christian enters prayer with the sincere intent of God's desire being the only desire of his heart. Fully confident that God delights in such a person, the Christian prays expectantly.

When these preconditions are sincerely in place, the Christian asks, seeks, and knocks in prayer. All three actions are in the present imperative tense in Greek. This means prayer is to be continuous until the result is reached. How long should a person pray over a specific issue? Until God answers (and the solution fits in with all the other things God is structuring) or until He clarifies that one is to stop praying about the matter.

Jesus asks His hearers a common-sense question concerning a father's response when the son requests him. This solidifies the Christian's assurance that God always responds wisely to the requests of His children. God always responds wisely and compassionately to prayer. In some cases, His answer is "No." Aren't you glad that some of the things for which you prayed, God denied? Again, have you not experienced the joy of recognizing that He answered, "Not now" and only later realized how much better His response was? Be assured God does not need to be coerced—He delights to respond when prayer aligns His will in heaven with His will on earth.

What does Jesus want me to know?

Why does He want me to know this?

What does He want me to do in response?

Day Thirty-Seven

"Therefore, whatever you want men to do to you, do also to them for this is the Law and the Prophets."

MATTHEW 7:12

The Golden Rule may be the best known—and least practiced—of Jesus' teaching. It is about as well known as "judge not" and as often violated. So simple in terminology, so profound in implication, the Golden Rule is something of the capstone of everything Jesus taught. One thing that makes it stand out is that there is no equivalent in any other world religion.

As we have often noted in our study of the Sermon on the Mount, the wisest Jewish rabbis often taught things like what Jesus taught. The difference was, usually, that Jesus went well beyond the rabbis' teaching. The rabbis taught something like the Golden Rule only in the negative. "Don't do to another what you wouldn't want them to do to you." How was Jesus' teaching so unique? Doesn't the negative Golden Rule the rabbis taught mean the same thing? Not at all!

Consider the difference of a person obeying traffic laws. Such laws define how to drive safely—right side of the road, no passing in marked zones, obey the speed limit, etc. This, not only to avoid being hurt oneself but to not hurt someone else. Don't do __ because someone might get hurt or killed. This is a good thing, but so limited.

Now, think how different the positive Golden Rule is. As you are driving, and see another person with a car breakdown on the side of the road. Stop and help. If you see someone out of gas, go to the nearest station, get gas, and take it to them. Such a practice is the Golden Rule. It is not so much what you don't do as much as what you do. It costs you time, effort, perhaps money. What if you were out of gas, had car trouble? Wouldn't you hope someone would care enough (*agape*) to help?

Once again, we see the blessed thread of true Christianity on display. This "thread" runs through all Jesus taught. Blessed are those who gladly display God's character by giving practical, loving expression of it in daily living. We see the Golden Rule in action from the beatitudes, though judging wisely and compassionately. Love acts. Yes, it can cost you. It can be inconvenient. Perhaps someone else really should do it. No matter. Recognize a need, meet it, expect nothing in return. That is the Golden Rule.

Most people practice the negative version. It is so much easier to move over a lane on the highway to avoid possibly injuring a stranded motorist. It is easier to say, "They have a family. Their family should be helping them. It is easier to hand a person a couple of dollars than to take the time to know and respond to the real story. That's it: "most people" versus the actual Golden Rule person.

What does Jesus want me to know?

Why does He want me to know this?

What does He want me to do in response?

Day Thirty-Eight

"Enter by the narrow gate; for wide is the gate and broad is the way that leads to destruction, and there are many who go in by it. Because narrow is the gate and difficult is the way which leads to life, and there are a few that find it."

MATTHEW 7:13-14

Sooner or later, every person faces a crossroad. There, a decision has to be made. Now, they are seeing where their choice is taking them. Such is life. Some intersections are relatively minor: "What shall I have for lunch?" Some are major: "Is this the person I am to marry?" Some are eternal: "What will you do with Jesus?" Decisions. There is a timeless principle: For every choice, there is a consequence. What you sow, you reap.

Once again, Jesus continues to teach with the "blessed thread," continuing to tie all of life together. Be wise in the decisions you make at the crossroads of life. Moses (Deuteronomy 30:15-20), Joshua (Joshua 24:15), and Jeremiah (Jeremiah 21:8) are examples of those who recognized the reality: Crossroads are inevitable; be ready.

This summarizes Jesus' teaching concerning the crossroad decisions people make.

1. Only two ultimate choices determine one's eternal destiny: surrender to Jesus or refuse to do so. That's it. Eternity will be the outcome of your decision. Most choose not to surrender to Jesus. They just live in this present world and do nothing regarding eternity.

2. The choice is the easy way or the hard way. The easy way is just that easy. It is natural, requires no effort, and is entirely satisfactory in the short term. But in the long term, such a choice is disastrous beyond belief. At the end of the broad (easy) road, there is hell.

3. To not choose is to choose. It was once said, "The only thing necessary for the triumph of evil is for good men to do nothing" (Incorrectly attributed to Edmund Burke. Similar statements are found in literature). You will get run over if you stand in indecision at a crossroad. You have no choice but to choose.

4. It is inescapable—the hard way is hard. One cannot succeed apart from work, hard work. To be a concert pianist requires long hours of practice every day. The top athlete must develop a disciplined work ethic—common sense. Nothing of value is easy. Thomas Gray's *Elegy Written in a Country Churchyard*" took eight years to perfect. Coleridge was a genius in thought, but little of his brilliance ever made it to paper. He could never discipline himself to write down what he felt and saw. Surrendering to Jesus is not physically hard surrendering one's demand to be one's own master is hard.

One of Satan's most effective strategies is "Someday...not today." Everyone acknowledges death is inevitable. Eternity is coming, but I will deal with that later, not today. Crossroads. One leads to eternal death; it is easy...for now. The other leads to eternal life; it is demanding...for now. Which road are you on?

What does Jesus want me to know?

Why does He want me to know this?

What does He want me to do in response?

Day Thirty-Nine

"Beware of false prophets, who come to you in sheep's clothing, but inwardly they are ravenous wolves. You will know them by their fruits. Do men gather grapes from thornbushes or figs from thistles? Even so, every good tree bears good fruit, but a bad tree bears bad fruit. A good tree cannot bear bad fruit, nor can a bad tree bear good fruit. Every tree that does not bear good fruit is cut down and thrown into the fire. Therefore, by their fruits, you will know them."

MATTHEW 7:15-20

Hypocrites, how Jesus loathed them! At the top of His list were the religious hypocrites. Again and again, He confronted the professional hypocrites—the Pharisees. Through all the ages, false prophets have been active and the source of much mischief. Wolves in sheep's clothing, Jesus called them. Ezekiel denounced them (Ezekiel 22:27); Paul warned about them in the New Testament (Acts 20:29). The shepherds wore sheepskins with the fleece turned inside. Reversed, and with a bit of ingenuity, the skin could be stretched over the body to look like a wolf. The American Indians sometimes disguised their appearance with wolf skins in their buffalo hunts. False prophets were skilled in disguising themselves. Wearing a prophet's distinctive mantle, speaking prophet-like messages in a prophet-like tone, they deceived many. But watch them closely, and soon their true character will appear.

The *Didache*, completed about A.D. 100, was the first book to regulate the practices of early Christians. Ample space was given to false prophets and the things that would expose their falsehood. False prophets, according to the *Didache*, could be identified by:

1. **Teaching for personal gain**—The prophet's ministry was unique and very helpful to the cause of Christ. Men specially called of God and gifted by Him helped ground the early church in practices that advanced God's kingdom (Ephesians 4:11). The office was highly respected within the church. These men taught from place to place in an intenerate ministry and fulfilled their calling. They trusted God for their support, and they were well supported. Seeing the financial support the prophets received for what they perceived to be an undemanding task; false prophets began to travel among the churches. They never finished teaching without asking for support.

To receive greater offerings, the false prophets learned to "read" an audience and determine what "message" would be most lucrative. Many were able to craft their hypocrisy most convincingly. The result was not a message from God but a message that would prolong their stay at a church and gain the greatest reward from churches which "paid well."

2. **Seeking prestige**—As already mentioned, true prophets were highly respected both in their office and for their ministry's benefit to the churches. Because they were so highly respected,

their message (even when it was contentious, and painful) was valued and was usually obeyed. Their message was unique and their time with any given church was limited. Prophets did not have to deal with the daily details that the pastor/teacher had to contend with. They traveled, saw new things, met new people, and the money was decent.

All of this was quite appealing to the false prophets. Honestly, the prophet could be the laziest person in town. If he spoke well, turned on the appropriate emotion at the right time, and was reasonably good at crowd psychology, he could work up a few impressive speeches, memorize them, learn good fundraising appeals, and do quite well. When he sensed he had collected about all he could hope for from a given congregation, he would move on and repeat the cycle in the next church. Oh, the days before social media! "Read" the new church, add or delete a few sentences from their speech, receive the admiration and money that poured in... what a cushy job!

3. **It was a message of their concoction**—Several false prophets had a specific agenda. They cobbled together a few proof texts, some high-sounding phrases, and a powerful, persuasive manner to gain traction and a following in a church. This was a particular temptation in a church that "paid well". Not only was it financially lucrative, but it also provided the opportunity to become known. The result was that much division and turmoil were created in the churches because many were deceived. These false prophets were able messengers of their father, the devil.

The early church fathers detected false prophets, and the *Didache—The Teaching of the Twelve* resulted. This provided guidance for the churches concerning the false prophet menace.

A true prophet never remained with a church for more than two days. He was not a true prophet if he stayed three or more days. He never asked for more than bread. If he asked for money, he was not a true prophet. The crowning proof was simply if what he prophesied accorded with Scripture and was consistent with his character and practice; he was a true prophet. This also included his working at a trade to support himself if necessary.

This brings us to the expression, "...by their fruits, you will know them" (Matthew 7:15-20). Evil root, bad fruit. One's message is rooted in his character and standing with his god. If God (Jehovah) is one's God, his nature and practice will show it—consistently—as a way of life. If one's god is himself and how his god can help him achieve his desires, that is the message he delivers.

So, what about the fruit of the false prophet? As time goes on, several expressions of "fruit" will appear:

1. His message will require little sacrifice—it will be easy, appealing. "All you have to do is... God is a God of grace... Do what makes you happy...If you get caught in "sin" He is gracious to forgive you, so just say "I'm sorry," and all is well." Paul confronted this forcefully in Romans 6.

2. His message will focus primarily on externals—following the letter of the law. His message is that you are fine if you cross the "T's" and dot the "I's". The Pharisees adopted this message in a complete way, better than any others ever have.

Jesus denounced the Pharisees more than any other people on earth.

3. Negatives will dominate his message. Abstain from ___, and _____ and _____. Little regard was given to what one does. Since a negative religion can never be pinned down (How much "not" is enough?), each person becomes their judge. Therefore, whatever the individual decided was right was final.

4. He will emphasize separation. In extreme cases, false prophets emphasized withdrawal from social engagement. Isolation from the marketplace, from social engagement, and the ascetic life in the desert or on a mountain top, was ideal, according to the false prophet. Interestingly enough, few of them did so...it was too costly.

5. The message of the false prophet produced a holier-than-thou attitude. Adherents were the elite in their own opinion. They were far above those ordinary ones who simply considered it valid Christianity to live out their convictions in the workplace. When these ordinary Christians sinned, they repented, confessed their sin, and purposed not to do it again. The holier-than-thou group felt that was too much trouble. After all, God is a God of grace and forgiveness. A simple "I'm sorry" was enough; no need for all that repenting, confessing, etc.

Yes, give careful attention to both the message and the messenger's character. Their fruits will reveal their true identity. Indeed, by their fruits, you shall know them.

What does Jesus want me to know?

Why does He want me to know this?

What does He want me to do in response?

Day Forty

"Not everyone who says to me, Lord, Lord, shall enter the kingdom of heaven, but he who does the will of My Father in heaven. Many will say to Me in that day, Lord, Lord, have we not prophesied in your name, cast out demons in your name, and done many wonders in your name? And then I will declare to them, I never knew you; depart from Me, you who practice lawlessness!"

MATTHEW 7:21-23

Words are easy to memorize. "The Sinner's Prayer" can be repeated by a child. Talk is cheap. The real issue is the genuineness of the heart, the spring out of which words flow (Matthew 12:34). It's sad that so many who say the right words are deceived into believing that "repeating the formula" puts them in right standing with God.

Today, almost all people believe they will go to heaven when they die. If pressed for the basis of their conviction, they will almost always speak of their works. They are sure that they do more good than bad, so when their life is weighed on God's balance scale, they are satisfied they will be okay.

Good works are commendable and should always be encouraged. A positive attitude and a willingness to help, even sacrificing to do so, make the world a more pleasant place. However, Jesus points out in these verses that as attractive, even miraculous as a lifestyle, it is not enough. Only the life that has been transformed by the new birth and motivated by a genuine faith—a life surrendered to Jesus—gains the approval of God.

Words, even behavior, cannot substitute for a new nature. Sooner or later the true nature will resurface. A day of reckoning is coming. God always looks at the heart. The layers of good works, commendable as they may be, will be stripped away one day to expose the heart. How utterly devastating to hear, "I never knew you."

What does Jesus want me to know?

Why does He want me to know this?

What does He want me to do in response?

Day Forty-One

"Therefore whoever hears these sayings of mine, and does them, I will liken him to a wise man who built his house on a rock; and the rain descended, the floods came, and the winds blew and beat on that house; and it did not fall, for it was founded on the rock. But everyone who hears these sayings of Mine, and does not do them, will be like a foolish man who built his house on the sand; and the rain descended, the floods came, and the winds blew and beat on that house; and it fell and great was its fall."

MATTHEW 7:24-27

Once again, we note the blessed "thread" that runs through all that Jesus taught. From the beginning of the Sermon on the Mount to the end, one thread dominates, and we see it summarized in these concluding verses. All that has been taught is illustrated in a wonderfully graphic but straightforward way.

The direct connection to the previous verses is obvious. Jesus, the Carpenter, speaks of the most critical part of all of his teaching. The most critical part of this illustration is the foundation. The craftsmanship of both builders appears to be the same. It is not the design of the building or the quality of the builder's skills that is at issue. Everything in the story is equal except for the site of the foundation.

Throughout Israel, some streams are dry except in the rainy season. The stream bed is smooth, easy to dig, and seems to be the ideal building site...in the dry season. If one only looks at the immediate details of the building site, the place to build is obvious. But, if you take a long look, you know the rainy season is coming. At some point, the storms will turn the soft, comfortable stream beds into torrents of floodwaters. The crashing flash flood will smash against the house built on sand. Soon the sand erodes, and the beautifully constructed house crashes and is washed away.

The builder who considers the immediate and the long term will give greater attention to the building site. He will do the hard work of digging down to bedrock and lay his foundation there. Floods of equal ferocity struck both houses. Both houses were equally well built. Both were tested. The foundation upon which the building rested made the difference.

"Therefore..." Since the first word of the sermon in Chapter 5:2, we have been on a be line to these concluding words. Notice how simple they are "...whoever hears these sayings of mine AND DOES THEM..." There you have it: hear (trust in, believe in, surrender to) the message, and then live out the message in the marketplace based on this foundation: love God and love people.

What does Jesus want me to know?

Why does He want me to know this?

What does He want me to do in response?

Day Forty-Two

"And so it was, when Jesus had ended these sayings, that the people were astonished at His teaching, for He taught them as one having authority, and not as the scribes."

MATTHEW 7:28-29

It's no wonder the people were astonished when Jesus finished His teaching. We are too! So simple, yet so profound. The whole of Jesus' life is revolutionary. Wherever His message has been heard and obeyed, lives have been totally remade; entire cultures have been radically transformed.

> But we never can prove the delights of His love
> Until all, on the altar, we lay.
> For the grace that He shows and joy He bestows
> Is for them who trust and obey![22]

With the Apostle John, we say in awe, "What a wonder that we should be called the children of God" (I John 3:1). Your summary response to what God has shown you in the study of the Sermon on the Mount...

It would be wise of you—and me—to go back and work through the entire Sermon on the Mount every six months. Done earnestly, we will profit for time and eternity.

What does Jesus want me to know?

Why does He want me to know this?

What does He want me to do in response?

About the Author

For over fifty years, Burtis Williams has served churches in the West Texas area as Minister of Youth, Minister of Education, Associate Pastor, and Pastor. He has also been a church planter and had a Christian counseling practice for over twenty-five years. For the past eleven years, he has served as Chaplain/Bereavement Coordinator for a hospice organization.

Burtis and his wife, Linda, are longtime residents of West Texas. They have two sons, five grandchildren, and two great-grandsons. In addition, they have two house cats and an assortment of stray cats and wildlife who appear at feeding time. He enjoys gardening, sports of all kinds, hunting, fishing, and writing. His greatest joy is found in helping people. His prayer is that God will be pleased to use the investment He has made in the author to bring others to Jesus while encouraging fellow Christians in their journey.

Endnotes

1 Toplady, Thomas. *Rock of Ages*. Public Domain.

2 Decision Magazine, vol. 42, Apr. 2001, pp. 4-5.

3 Askew, Thomas. "Judson, Adoniram" Evangelical Dictionary of World Missions. pp. 528-29. Edward Judson. *The Life of Adoniram Judson.*

4 Morgan, R. J. *On This Day*. Nashville: Nelson. 1997.

5 Comfort, G. A. "Wesley, Charles" Who's Who in Christian History. pp. 708-09.

6 Crosby, Fannie. *An Autobiography*. Grand Rapids. Baker. 1996.

7 Colson, Charles. *Born Again*. Old Tappan, N.J. Spire. 1977.

8 *Sweet By and By*—words by S.F.Bennet, music by J.P. Webster.

9 Hefley, James ad Marti Hefley. *By Their Blood: Christian Martyrs of the Twentieth Century.* 2nd Edition. Grand Rapids. Baker. 1996. pp. 500-501.

10 Wellman, Sam. "Corrie Ten Boom" in *Faith's Great Heroes*. Edited by David Lemdstedt. Ubricksville: Barbour. 1989.

11 Pollock, John. *John Wesley*, Victor, 1992.

12 "When I Survey the Wondrous Cross"—words by Isaac Watts; arranged by L. Mason.

13 Wellman, Sam. "Corrie Ten Boom" in *Faith's Great Heroes*. Edicted by David Lemdstedt. Ubricksville: Barbour. 1989.

14 Lofts, Norah. Ann Boleyn. New York: Coward, McCann and Geoghegan, Inc. 1979.

15 Agrant. M. "Renwick, James" Dictionary *of Scottish Church History and Theology*. pp. 709-710.

16 Wolfe, Hans Julius. *Marriage Law and Family Organization in Ancient Athens*, Cambridge University Press, 1944, p. 43.

17 "John Wesley and Women" Christian History Magazine. pp. 125-127.

18 Rustin, Michael and Sharon. The One-Year Book of Christian History. Tyndale, 2003, pp. 558-559.

19 Fleming, Thomas J. *One Small Candle: the Pilgrim's First Year in America*. New York: Norton. 1964. pp. 160-174.

20 Muller, George. A Narrative of Some of the Lord's Dealings with George Muller. 7th ed, London: Nisbet, 1869. pp. 143-307.

21 Criswell, W. A. *Standing on the Promises*, Dallas, Word, 1990.

22 Sammis, J.H. "Trust and Obey." Hope Publishing Company, owner, 1921.

Other Sources Consulted

International Standard Bible Encyclopedia

Church History Magazine

Dictionary of Christian Biography

The Story of Civilization by Will and Ariel Durant

New Schaff-Herzog Encyclopedia of Religious Knowledge

The International Dictionary of the Christian Church

Dictionary of Scottish Church History and Theology

Expositor's Bible Dictionary

Zondervan Pictorial Encyclopedia of the Bible

Strong's Exhaustive Concordance of the Bible

Made in the USA
Coppell, TX
29 January 2022

72632233R10125